GOD HAS A PLAN

BY STEVE HARROP

GOD HAS A PLAN

Copyright © 2025

All rights reserved. No part of this book may be reproduced in any form without permission in writing from the publisher. Thank you for supporting this author by complying with copyright laws.

Unless otherwise indicated, all scripture quotations are taken from the King James Bible version. www.biblegateway.com used with permission.

Verses marked AMP are taken from the AMP Bible (The Amplified Version). www.biblegateway.com used with permission.

Verses marked ESV are taken from the ESV Bible (The New English Standard Version). www.biblegateway.com used with permission.

Verses marked NIV are taken from the NIV Bible (The New International Version). www.biblegateway.com used with permission.

Verses marked NLT are taken from the NLT Bible (The New Living Translation). www.biblegateway.com used with permission.

Verses marked TPT are taken from the TPT Bible (The Passion Translation). www.biblegateway.com used with permission.

Printed in the United States of America

ISBN: 978-0-9914226-5-4

GOD HAS A PLAN

BY STEVE HARROP

TABLE OF CONTENTS

	FOREWARD	07
	INTRODUCTION	09
1	THE GOD OF VISION	11
2	PURE VISION	25
3	GOD PREPARES THE VISIONARY	37
4	VISION WITH STRATEGY	53
5	VISION AND FAITH	67
6	VISION OPERATES THROUGH FAITH	81
7	VISIONARY LEADERS	93
8	HINDRANCES TO VISION	105
9	CASTING THE VISION	119
10	ATTRACTIVE VISION	133
11	THE SYNERGY OF VISION	147
12	VISION'S REWARD	157
	ACKNOWLEDGMENTS	168
	SUGGESTED FURTHER READING	169
	NOTES	170

FOREWARD

I'm sure you have read many books on vision, but I don't think you'll ever read one quite like this one. Dr. Harrop covers the subject of vision from the ethereal to the moment the groundbreaking shovel goes into the ground and everything in between and beyond.

I've had the privilege of watching the development of the vision he describes from a close-up perspective and also from a distance. Most people think of a vision as something external. It is not until that vision becomes internal and an integral part of who we are that it ever comes to fruition. I've come to fully understand that in the years I've known Dr. Harrop and observed how that internalized vision has become an external reality through his consistency of faith, prayer, and passion for the call and purpose God has placed in his life.

As he says in this book, he is an encourager, which I translate to mean an exhorter, a modern- day Barnabas reaching out to those needing to hear the gospel and have a change in their lives. This spiritual DNA is not only in Pastor Harrop, but it is in the very soul of Cornerstone Full Gospel Church.

I'm convinced this latest book by Dr. Harrop will sow the seeds of vision into the lives of many people who will accomplish things that no one thought they could. Read until you reach the last period and then expect to be changed. I have!

Dr. Charles Travis

Founder/President Aidan University

and Logos Global Network

INTRODUCTION

Vision is a wonderful gift from God. Eyesight enables us to see everything around us. We are able to see the majestic handiwork of God's marvelous creation. From the wonders of the sky, to the diversity of the animal kingdom, we are able to enjoy creation because of the wonderful ability of sight. The gift of beholding that newborn baby and watching every precious facial expression cannot be articulated, it must be seen!

However, there is another vision that many people struggle to understand and experience. That is vision to see into our future, the wonderful plans of God. Every human being has been divinely designed by our Creator for His purposes. God's vision of eternity past, present, and future enables Him to see our mission in life long before we are conceived. It is amazing, even breathtaking to think of God's vision for creation and that He planned for us to have a part in it. Then to top it all off, the Lord shows us His plan and how we fit into His kingdom. That is what we call biblical vision. Jesus said the Holy Spirit would show us things to come. He said all that the Father shows Me I have made known to you. There is no need for the believer to walk in the dark. We are God's children, and He delights in revealing His plans to us.

You may think you are the most unlikely candidate for the Lord to call to fulfill His purposes. I thought the same thing. No one in my class at school would have chosen me, not my teachers, classmates, or even me. He chooses the most unlikely person, so He gets all of the glory.

You have been designed for greatness. The world may have programmed you for defeat. I encourage you to seek the Lord with all of your heart and ask Him for a clear vision of His will for your life. When He begins to give you glimpses of your future, stay humble, walk it out, and He will reveal the big picture in His time.

It is my prayer that *God Has A Plan* will inspire you to believe that God has a marvelous plan for your life and will help you fulfill your journey.

THE GOD OF VISION

CHAPTER ONE

"And it shall come to pass in the last days, saith God, I will pour out of my Spirit upon all flesh: and your sons and your daughters shall prophesy, and your young men shall see visions, and your old men shall dream dreams. And on my servants and on my handmaidens I will pour out in those days of my Spirit; and they shall prophesy" (Acts 2:17-18).

I had never really considered the full impact vision has on people until I attended a conference with some friends. We were discussing which breakout sessions to attend. A youth pastor from another church spoke up and said, "I would like to hear someone speak on vision." I had taken for granted the influence vision has on people and ministry. From my conversion through the past 49 years of serving Christ, I have experienced God's leading through His visions.

It is the heart of the Father that we know Him and His plan for our lives. When we need a clear understanding of what to do, He speaks in a way we know it is Him. Without visions and dreams, the church has no future or purpose. The Holy Spirit knows all and reveals the plans of the kingdom to us as partners. He causes us to see things that are not, but one day will be. Vision is the language of the Spirit. We are in the last days and God is speaking through visions, dreams, signs, and wonders.

My first vision came when I needed it to take the first step toward God by giving my life to Jesus Christ. For three weeks, I wanted to respond to the altar call, but I felt like there were unmovable lead weights on both feet. The night my breakthrough came, the preacher had spoken on the straight and narrow way in Matthew 7:13-14. It seemed as though somebody had told her my life's story of sin and shame. That night was different. I nearly ran to the altar. I prayed for at least 30 minutes trying to remember every sin and repent of each one; the list seemed to be endless. All at once, in my mind's eye but with eyes closed, I saw an image of Jesus hanging on the cross. I watched a drop of blood drip from His body. My eyes followed that drop of blood as it fell in slow motion and landed on the top of somebody's head. That somebody was me. At that moment I knew that one drop of Jesus' blood had cleansed me of every sin. What is hard to figure out is the fact that I didn't recall that vision until months later. One thing I do know is I really needed that vision from God that night. After that vision, I would never doubt the power of Jesus' precious blood.

I truly believe God provides visions that reveal His ultimate plan for your life. Jesus has a blueprint already designed just for you. The key to receiving it is faith and obedience. We'll talk more about that later. God's blueprint is revealed one page at a time. The blueprints for our church sanctuary are at least 30 pages long. You only follow one page at a time. The architect and contractor see the whole set of blueprints and the finished building, but the subcontractors just see one page at a time. We see the big picture of the vision of our lives, but it is revealed one stage at a time. The Master Architect of our lives knows what we need and when we need it. God is so gracious to reveal to us bite-size portions of the vision. If we knew the whole process of what it would take to fulfill the vision, it would overwhelm most of us.

Tom Thompson, a close friend of about 30 years, was driving down the highway when the Lord gave him a vision for The Refuge Ministry. The Lord showed him a vision of an isolated rural farm where addicts could come to escape their lives, break free of addiction, and learn to walk with God. In 1999 Tom founded The Refuge Ministry to help addicts get clean and sober by identifying and addressing the spiritual brokenness that underlies their addictions. The ministry applies a faith-based approach to treatment. The Refuge has helped over 4,000 men shake off the shackles of addiction in order to transform into better citizens, sons, husbands, and fathers. Tom is still growing the vision and expanding the ministry through the successful recovery model. The vision was so much bigger than Tom realized at the time. It had such an impact on him that he and his wife, Johna, sold their house and moved to Vinton County where they bought a farm and started The Refuge Ministry. It was a faith walk for the Thompson family. The vision the Lord gave Tom has never waned in his heart.[1]

Many people struggle with knowing what vision is and understanding how it works. Visions were something new to me until God began to unfold His plans through visions. Six months after I was saved I was awakened in the middle of the night by a nightmare. While I was fighting to get awake, the picture of Jesus hanging on the wall at the foot of the bed came alive. When my eyes fixed on the picture, Jesus turned around and knelt with His hands folded in prayer for a short time. Then He stood and gestured with His hands as He pivoted side-to-side as though He was speaking to a multitude of people. Next, He knelt back down to pray and then stood up to speak again. My eyes never blinked as the scene unfolded. They began to burn, so I blinked and the picture was back to normal hanging on the wall. Then sleep returned for the rest of the night.

The next day I told my wife, Pat, about the event. We questioned the vision and its meaning. It was a mystery to both of us. Pat told Aunt Trixie and she asked our pastor what the vision meant. He said he wasn't sure, but he noted that God would eventually reveal the purpose of the experience. Later the understanding was revealed. The Lord was saying as I pray to the Father His power would be released through the preaching of His Word. I have found that to be true.

So, what is a good definition of vision? It is God painting a picture of what our future is going to look like and the task He has planned for us. Vision gives a snapshot of the future. Vision gives direction and guidance toward the desired target. Vision will provide energy and passion to pursue and accomplish the goal. Vision sees a more desirable future, provides direction, and fuels motivation for its achievement.

GOD'S VISION

God does nothing spontaneously. He has a master plan for everything in the universe and for eternity. His "suddenlies" were planned out before the creation of time. The plan for a redeemed race of people was birthed in the heart of God before He created the earth. Revelation 21:27 states: "And there shall in no wise enter into it any thing that defileth, neither whatsoever worketh abomination, or maketh a lie: but they which are written in the Lamb's book of life." When Adam and Eve sinned in the Garden of Eden, it did not catch God off guard. He had already made plans for provision to redeem mankind: "Looking unto Jesus the author and finisher of our faith; who for the joy that was set before Him endured the cross, despising the shame, and is set down at the right hand of the throne of God" (Hebrews 12:2). The New International Version (NIV) explains Christ as, "the pioneer and perfector of our faith." Thus, "for this purpose the Son of God was manifested, that He might destroy the works of the devil" (1 John 3:8b). It is obvious the plan of salvation was well thought out in the visionary heart and mind of God. Not only does He have a plan for all of mankind, but He also has a plan for every individual. He has a vision of where we fit in His kingdom because God is omniscient, all- knowing of everything past, present, and future.

    Little did I know of all He had planned for my life. However, when I was two years of age, my Grandpa Harrop knew of God's plan for me. Grandpa had cancer and every Sunday Mom, Dad, my older brother Junior, and I would go visit him. Every week Grandpa would take me on his lap and tell Mom and Dad that I would be a preacher one day. It was the Lord showing Grandpa His vision for my life. Just weeks before I became a true believer in Jesus Christ as my Savior and Lord Mom told me what Grandpa had said.

However, confirmation would be needed. It seemed like every place I went, someone would ask, "Are you going to be a preacher?" About a year and a half later, while praying for people at the altar in our church, the Lord spoke to my spirit as clear as a bell that He wanted me to preach His Word. That night, I settled it in my heart and mind that this was God's plan for my life. At 24 years of age, having never read the Bible through, and struggling with public speaking, I surrendered to whatever the Lord wanted me to do. It would take years of preparation to get ready. By God's grace, I had to learn how to read all over again because reading had always been difficult for me.

THE POWER OF VISION

While here on earth, Jesus was empowered by vision. We are to follow after Him and to be led by the Holy Spirit. John 5:19b states, "The Son can do nothing of himself, but what He seeth the Father do..." And John 5:30 reveals, "I can of mine own self do nothing: as I hear, I judge: and judgment is just; because I seek not mine own will, but the will of the Father which hath sent me." The Father is constantly revealing His will and plan for us. All we must do is seek Him with our whole heart and He will unfold His purposes to us. To seek Him is to find Him. Open your mind and spirit to Him and you will receive vision in His unique way. He is the God of visions and dreams.

Vision is so powerful that Nathanael doubted Philip had met the Christ in John 1:48a. "Jesus answered and said unto him, Before that Philip called thee, when thou wast under the fig tree, I saw thee" (John 1:48). In verse 49, "Nathanael answered and saith unto him, Rabbi, thou art the Son of God; thou art the King of Israel." Jesus divinely saw Nathaneal when he knew nobody was around. Being able to receive vision from the Father opens the door of the supernatural to ministry.

So many believers say, "I never have visions" or "God doesn't speak to me." God said that in the last days, "Your young men shall see visions" (Acts 2:17c). Ask Him to speak to you through visions and dreams. Jesus said in John 10:27, "My sheep hear My voice, and I know them, and they follow me." I am a firm believer that God wants to communicate with His children constantly. Learn to hear the voice of the Good Shepherd. He speaks in many different ways. It seems as though the Lord uses dreams and visions to confirm what He has already been speaking to us.

When I was planning to go to Florida for two weeks to write this book, trouble filled my spirit. One night, the Lord showed up in a dream in which a Christian friend spoke to me and said, "Don't go to Florida and write." I woke up and my wife, Pat, was already up. I went to her and told her about the dream. She said she had felt uneasy about the Florida trip, but hadn't said anything. The trip was canceled. On the day before we were scheduled to leave, my accountability partner had to cancel because of a death in his congregation. The next week, our son was diagnosed with a mass on his right kidney and was scheduled to have the kidney removed. My heart was thankful for the Lord's guidance. It took a vision in a dream to stop me from going to Florida for two weeks so we could be home with our son and all of our family.

Dale Galloway believes that vision is seeing into the future through God's revealed plan and vision before it exists. Vision is a mental picture that gives you a clear direction for the future.[2] Vision enables God's people to walk according to His plan and purpose. Without vision we stumble and lose our way. Proverbs 29:18 states, "Where there is no vision, the people perish." Where there is no redemptive revelation from God, the people go astray. Vision from heaven keeps us on the straight and narrow. Abram received revelation from heaven in Genesis 15:5, "Look now toward the heaven, and tell the stars, if thou be able to number them: and He said unto him, so shall thy seed be." The power of vision gave an unlimited promise to Abram. Never limit God. Dream big because we serve a big God that has all power: "Now unto Him that is able to do exceedingly abundantly above all that we ask or think, according to the power that worketh in us" (Ephesians 3:20).

Galloway tells a story about a fisherman catching nothing while a couple nearby were throwing the big ones back. "Finally, ...he yelled, 'How come you're throwing the big ones back?' The couple reached under the seat of the boat and pulled out a small frying pan. They answered, 'Cause they won't fit in our frying pan.'"[3] What an example of people who God gives big dreams and visions, but they're dwarfed thinking only sees their limitations. That type of thinking limits God by their tiny faith. It's time to enter the land of visions and dreams with God. When we do, life is changed from natural reason to supernatural living. When we pray based on the supernatural power of vision, we know our prayers are answered. People of vision have no trouble believing in God. Hebrews 11:1 (NIV) says, "Now faith is confidence in what we hope for and assurance about what we do not see." Hebrews 11:6 continues, "And without faith it is impossible to please God."

THE POWER OF VISION EQUALS THE TASK

God is always faithful to give the visionary a vision that is equal to the task He has called them to perform. The bigger the task, the greater the need for powerful, detailed vision. When God called Moses to the mammoth task of delivering the Hebrews out of Egyptian bondage, He gave him convincing visions. First, He showed Moses a burning bush that was not consumed by fire and then He spoke to him face-to-face. Moses was able to cling to the burning bush encounter for future encouragement. If that wasn't enough, God caused Moses' hand to become leprotic and then clean again. He caused his rod to turn into a snake and then back to a rod again. The Lord told him he would use his rod to turn the water of the Nile River into blood and to do other signs as well (see Exodus 3-4). The bigger the task, the greater the need for giant-sized revelations from God.

THE VISION IN 1986

In the early spring of 1986, I was attending a prayer meeting. The stirring of God had not stopped for a whole year. God had given me great contentment while serving as an assistant pastor at Trinity Full Gospel Church for five years. My pastor of ten years was very good to me, and he believed in me. He was a true spiritual father. He had shared many times that I would be the next pastor of Trinity Full Gospel Church. I took him at his word and believed that to be true.

The only thing missing was the fact that the Lord had never told me that. Hence, the divine dissatisfaction. I loved my job and the people, but the Lord had slowly been weaning my heart from my home church. After the prayer meeting, I went home and found that Pat was already in bed, but I was still not yet able to retire for the day. It was about 2:00 a.m. when I knelt at the chair in the living room and began to pray. God had something to show me. With my eyes closed, I earnestly prayed, "Lord, what do you want me to do?" Having prayed that prayer many times that year, all at once I was overlooking Duncan Falls from an aerial view. A church stood in the middle of what was a cornfield at that time. I was unable to describe the building because a golden light encompassed the building and was reflecting in all directions. It was obvious the light was the glory of God. His presence would radiate from the church and then impact territories to the north, south, east, and west. Instantly the interpretation of the vision flooded my entire being. I asked the Lord, "Is that what you want me to do?" He replied, "Go for it." He spoke in a language a child could understand. The vision was so clear and profound that I have never doubted my call to Duncan Falls to preach the gospel.

Six weeks later we held our first worship services at the Duncan Falls American Legion Hall. The Legion members were so accommodating and kind to us that it was no doubt the favor of God. Many times, I have drawn on that vision for comfort and encouragement. It has been over 38 years since God gave me the vision that has produced numerous building projects, thousands of souls saved, and now a church of hundreds of hard-working, Christ-filled, loving people. To God be the glory for the great things He has done. The vision is still burning bright and clear, and God has confirmed the best days of ministry are yet ahead.

In 1985, the Lord brought a lady by the name of Doris Dew my way. She went home to be with the Lord a few years ago. Doris was one of the most gifted writers of poetry. After we started the church in 1986, she handed me this poem that sums up the vision of Cornerstone Full Gospel Church.

A Dream Come True
By Doris Dew[4]

A dream was born in the heart of a man, inspired by God above
He dreamed of a church in a great cornfield where people could worship and love.
This young man was walking hand in hand with the giver of life
He wanted a church to be known far and wide, a church without envy and strife.
It seemed that this place would never be, he had no way of knowing
That God was keeping the vision alive and the way He soon would be showing.
He had to start out all alone, the finances were not there
It seemed he was walking by himself and no one seemed to care.
He had no land and really no plan, but the vision would not die
So one day he simply said to the Lord "on you I must rely"
He left the place where he had been - a place that was safe and secure
It seemed he really had to go - if his soul would much longer endure.
He fought the battle and paid the price - I can tell you the price was great
It was hard to go on in a critical world, not being sure of his fate.
But he had many friends, supplied by God, who would go the last mile with him
Who would help and pray both night and day when his faith would grow kind of dim.
So with prayers and tears and hope and faith, all put together with love,
You will see this church where the cornfield was, it is smiled on by God above.
You are always welcome and there you will find hope when you're all alone
Where we love one another and God most of all — the church is called "Cornerstone."

There are volumes of testimonies of people who have had visions and those visions walked out have impacted the world. Maybe you have heard of the movie "Field of Dreams." Ray Kinsella had missed out on his dreams as a baseball player. He lived in Iowa on his farm with a large cornfield. He heard voices saying, "If you build it (a ballpark in the cornfield), they will come." So, he did, and they came. That movie alone has inspired untold millions of people to follow their dreams to their fruition.[5]

I am an encourager by nature. Encouraging people to pray and seek God's will for their lives is my greatest passion. Once a person discovers God's vision for their life, they can join hands with God and walk it out. There is nothing more fulfilling than knowing you are in step with your destiny. Destiny is the reason or purpose God created you. His vision is the template for you to follow His designed plan. So many people live their whole life unfulfilled, never discovering God's plan for them. Colonel Harland Sanders was almost one of those people. At age 65 he retired, yet was very unhappy and depressed. His wife suggested he take his famous chicken recipe, with 11 herbs and spices, on the road and build franchises across the country. He did just that, but the journey was not easy. He was rejected 1009 times before selling his first franchise. For the next 12 years he traveled the highways across the United States starting 600 franchises. He would later sell his company for two million dollars. Colonel Sanders is an example that it is never too late to follow your dream.[6]

The Demoniac of Gadara in Mark 5:1-20 is a perfect example of a man with no purpose. He was tormented day and night for years. When Jesus set him free from the demons that possessed him, he desired to join Jesus' ministry team. He probably envisioned Jesus preaching and him testifying about how he had no hope, no future, and then Jesus set him free. Jesus told the man He had a vision for him: go back home and tell your family and friends what great things had been done for you. The changed man went back to the region of Decapolis (having ten cities) and spread the good news. Jesus knew the future. He knew He would be preaching in Decapolis in the future. This man's testimony would plant seeds of the gospel in the people's hearts. When Jesus returned there would be a great harvest of souls.

Unlike the Demoniac, the country people begged Jesus to leave. They had no vision of what Jesus could do for their people. They couldn't see past the herd of swine they lost when the legion of demons entered them and then drowned the swine in the sea.

Learn to live your life with the expectation that God is setting up a domino effect for every stage of your life. You will see the fingerprints of God in every move. You might be in a dry place in your life, but in God's timing, things will begin to fall into place. God sees the big picture where you only see things in part. A commercial aired on TV some time ago. At first, it appeared a man was pulling a woman out of a car in an abduction attempt. When the camera widened the view, the real truth was revealed. The woman's car was on fire and the man was rescuing her from the flames. Sometimes what we can see of our lives looks dismal and bleak, when actually God is setting us up for our next great victory. The Red Sea looked pretty hopeless for the Hebrew children. God had a plan and a man to work the plan. God said to Moses, stretch your rod over the sea, stand still, and see the salvation of the Lord (see Exodus 14:13). When we stand with God's vision, the plan always comes together. God is truly the God of visions.

PURE VISION

CHAPTER TWO

"BLESSED ARE THE PURE IN HEART: FOR THEY SHALL SEE GOD" (MATTHEW 5:8).

A good friend of mine, a spiritual mentor, told me years ago that Cornerstone Church is the purest vision he had ever seen. It is very humbling to have that said about the church you pastor, especially from a man that I greatly respected. However, pure vision should be the goal of every pastor or ministry leader.

I believe Cornerstone is pure because it was birthed by the Lord Jesus Himself. Before it existed prophetic words were spoken in the mid-1960s. A group of Spirit-filled men stood on the corner of Main Street and Mill Street in Duncan Falls at the Gulf Service Station. These men included Pastor Harley Fidler, Bob Fountain, Carl Sullivan, and my great-uncle Loyd Emory. As they talked on that corner that day, the Spirit of the Lord came upon them, and they began to prophesy. The Lord said He was going to raise up a multi-faceted ministry in this area. A few blocks north on Mill Street, where it changes to Salt Creek Drive, is where Cornerstone Church is located. At that time, it was a cornfield waiting for its purpose to change. What really amazes me is the fact that those four visionary men had just left our farm after I had led them over the hills and valleys looking for rabbits. Little did I realize, or did they fathom, that the visionary of that church they saw in the Spirit would be me.

Grandpa Harrop had always dreamed of building a tabernacle on Back Run Road in Blue Rock. I believe the Lord had given Grandpa the vision as He did to David. But as Solomon would build the temple, so the Lord used the young boy hunting rabbits to build the church Grandpa saw in the location God would give the boy. It is so humbling to know the Lord chooses whom He will for His task.

"But God hath chosen the foolish things of the world to confound the wise; and God hath chosen the weak things of the world to confound the things which are mighty; and base things of the world, and things which are despised, hath God chosen, yea, and things which are not, to bring to nought things that are; that no flesh should glory in His presence" (1 Corinthians 1:27-29).

THE PURE IN HEART

Let's look at the Amplified Version (AMP) of Matthew 5:5. "Blessed [inwardly peaceful, spiritually secure, worthy of respect] are the gentle [the kind-hearted, the sweet-spirited, the self- controlled], for they will inherit the earth." The blessed have the integrity to do right when no one is watching. The gentle simply have the courage to display good morals and godly character. This courage comes when we are in union with

Christ.

Now let's look at Matthew 5:8 in The Passion Translation (TPT), "What bliss you experience when your heart is pure (full of innocence)! For then your eyes will open to see more and more of God." The Aramaic word used for "see" is "nahzon" and can be translated either in the present tense "they see God" or the future tense "they will see God." The Greek can be translated as "they will progressively see God." It's been said that the pure in heart will see visions from God now and will see God in heaven. How exciting to know that He reveals Himself to us in a progressive manner. The aim and goal are a pure heart.

PURE HEART - PURE MOTIVE

Many years ago, I heard Tommy Barnett, who has built two mega-churches, speak at a church conference. His passion and zeal for the Lord and souls set my soul ablaze. Tommy made a profound statement: "The only thing that could keep a church from growing is a wrong motive." Pure religion is a pure motive that shows up in caring for God's children. "Pure religion and undefiled before God and the Father is this, To visit the fatherless and widows in their affliction, and to keep himself unspotted from the world" (James 1:27).

We should always search our hearts for wrong motives. Nobody knows us better than we do. It's not just what we do, but why we do it that matters the most. Even the Pharisees in Jesus' day did good works but for the wrong motive - to be praised by man.

Authentic greatness is a result of following the directives of Jesus. Vision must hold to pure motives and refuse to compromise. Cornerstone Church has worked hard to maintain the integrity of the original mission statement. It was simple, yet profound. The statement is this:

> *Cornerstone Full Gospel Church exists to preach the Word, worship the Lord, win the lost, and make disciples to send locally and abroad.*

In chapter one, I introduced you to the poet Doris Dew. She was a faithful member of Cornerstone from the first day that we started the church. Doris was a pure-hearted lady who would serve behind the scenes, yet wanted no recognition. By 1988, my Bible was falling apart. I had so many notes and highlighted scripture in it that I needed to purchase the same Bible and transfer everything to my new one. I certainly didn't have time to do that so I asked Doris to do the transferring. She gladly agreed to do so, never telling one person - even though it took her 30 days to complete the task. She gladly presented it to me with everything identical to my old Bible. She was a true example of a pure heart with pure motives.

I'll never forget speaking with a pastor one day about his preaching. He said, "When I preach, I preach to the 5,000 people who are coming into the church." I asked, "What about the 15 people in attendance?" "I look over the top of them and preach to the 5,000 that are on their way," was his reply. I, on the other hand, believe a pure motive preaches only to those who are present.

Pure motives come from seeing God's will. I think some of the purest visions of a church plant are found in Acts 16:6-31. Paul was like a horse in the starting block of a race. He was chomping at the bit to preach the Word, but the Lord forbade him to preach in Asia. After they went to Mysia they tried to go to Bithynia, but the Holy Spirit would not let them go. They traveled to Troas and a vision appeared to Paul in the night. There stood a man of Macedonia asking him to come to Macedonia and help. Paul knew this was the Lord directing him. He and his comrade headed toward Phillippi. When they arrived, they heard of a group of women who were meeting at the river for prayer on the Sabbath. Lydia and her household became believers and were baptized. A church was planted in Phillippi that grew to be a mighty church of influence for the kingdom.

The church experienced rapid growth. A possessed slave girl was freed of her demons by Paul using the name of Jesus. The owners of the girl had Paul and Silas arrested, beaten, and thrown into jail. In jail, Paul and Silas continually prayed and sang praises to the Lord. Suddenly, the Lord sent an earthquake to open the prison and loosen their shackles. The jailor was about to kill himself when Paul intervened. The soldier and his entire house were saved.

This church at Phillippi was birthed out of vision. When we seek God with our whole heart and follow His leading, we position ourselves with heaven and will be led by pure vision. Paul and Silas' hearts were pure. They only wanted to glorify God with their gifting. God can and will use those who are pure in heart.

A pure heart is birthed in prayer that is centered on the Lord's perfect will. Asking the Lord to reveal my motive, mood, and method will lead to the Lord's will.[7] I call it praying the vision through. Had Paul been impatient and gone to the first city he came to, he would have missed the vision appointment the Lord had for him. The pure in heart will wait on the Commander in Chief for his marching orders. Lord, purify my heart so that I can hear from heaven and follow your vision.

When speaking of a pure heart, I think of King David. In Acts 13:22 God referred to David as a man after His own heart. Even though David had a moral blowout that cost him his family and the kingdom dearly, he never failed in Kingdom matters. First of all, he never led Israel into idolatry. Secondly, he submitted to the Lord's will concerning the building of the Temple. The Lord gave David the blueprint for the Temple and even the resources but would not permit him to build it. God instructed him to have his son, Solomon, build the Temple. David's heart was pure like his Heavenly Father's. A pure heart leads to pure vision. Ask the Lord to give you a pure heart that He may gift you with pure vision. Surrender everything to the Lord. When God gives us vision, we must give it back to Him and His Lordship. Anything God gives us, He wants to control. When God gave Abraham and Sarah a son, Isaac, in their old age, He later required Abraham to give Isaac back. Why would God require Abraham to offer Isaac? So that Abraham's heart would remain pure and he would not worship the gift God had given him. Abraham never hesitated, he was willing to sacrifice Isaac as the Lord commanded.

GOD PLACES PURE VISION IN OUR HEART

Pure vision is marinated with God Himself. Just like marinating a steak or chicken with a variety of herbs, spices, and oils to penetrate into the meat, we are to bathe ourselves in the presence of Jesus so the fruit of the Spirit will penetrate every fiber of our being. Our old character will be changed into the fragrant aroma and tasteful image of Jesus. This transformation is described by Galatians 5:22-23 (TPT), "But the fruit produced by the Holy Spirit within you is divine love in all its varied expressions: joy that overflows, peace that subdues, patience that endures, kindness in action, a life full of virtue, faith that prevails, gentleness of heart, and strength of spirit. Never set the Law above these qualities, for they are meant to be limitless." Spend time worshiping the Lord with good worship songs. In His presence, we are transitioned into His likeness. The purer the heart, the more vision God can entrust to you. He is in no hurry. Marinating takes time but the best cooks plan ahead for the process to be complete.

Allow God to work His character and the precious fruit of the Spirit to saturate you. God places pure vision in pure hearts. "But as it is written, eye hath not seen, nor ear heard, neither have entered into the heart of man, the things which God hath prepared for them that love Him. But God hath revealed them unto us by His Spirit: for the Spirit searches all things, yea, the deep things of God. For what man knoweth the things of a man, save the spirit of man that is in him? Even so, the things of God knoweth no man, but the Spirit of God" (1 Corinthians 2:9-11).

The Holy Spirit reveals pure visions to His beloved children.

PURE VISION OR ENVY?

Years ago, a good pastor friend told me of his encounter with God. The Lord asked him if it was okay if He didn't use him. Mark thought about that question and replied to the Lord, "Yes, Lord, just so the job gets done." Some people covet other people's vision. Another pastor friend came to see our first sanctuary which was built in 1989. He marveled at the beauty and congratulated me. Then he dropped a bomb by saying, "It's obvious God loves you more than He does me." I replied, "No, this is just the vision God gave me. He has given you a vision too, walk it out, and be thankful." We see the facilities God has given us as a tool to glorify God. We don't worship buildings or even visions. We worship God and thank Him for vision, which includes anything we need to expand the Kingdom of God.

Anything we do that has the slightest scent of envy takes on the stench of self. That odor will be detected by one and all. Many visions today are nothing more than envy.

> "The Apostle Paul lists envy as common as cornflakes among pastors, among (other) abhorrent sins. 'The acts of the sinful nature are obvious; sexual immorality, impurity, and debauchery; idolatry and witchcraft; hatred, discord, jealousy, fits of rage, selfish ambition, dissensions, factions and envy, drunkenness, orgies and the like' (Galatians 5:19-21). An ideal church is an idol;

a vision for ministry is a prophecy."[8]

So how do we rid ourselves of the sin of Cain which led to him murdering his brother? We must ask the Lord to search our hearts and see if there is any hidden sin. Ask yourself when visiting other churches: am I happy for them or is my heart filled with covetousness? The beauty in pure vision is the absence of selfishness and the cheerfulness in giving.

In 1988, Cornerstone Church did not have a church building. We rented the Philo High School Auditorium and the American Legion Hall. We were so thankful to have nice places in which to worship. At that time, Dr. Charles Travis asked me if we would like to help fund and build a church for a congregation in Juarez, Mexico. We as a church gladly joined Dr. Travis and another church in this project. It was my first mission trip. I know the Lord wanted me to experience the impoverished area of Juarez and the beautiful Mexican believers. Throughout the day we worked on the church structure, and in the evening held revival services. It was there that I met evangelist Chris Owensby. He was preaching the revival. I went to Mexico to bless the people, but the Lord blessed me with a lifetime friend in Chris.

Also, in February of 1989, we moved into our own church building. What Mike Murdock said is true, "What you make happen for others, God will make happen for you." It is the spiritual law of reciprocity: giving and receiving, "Be not deceived; God is not mocked: for whatsoever a man soweth, that shall he also reap" (Galatians 6:7). Similarly Luke tells us: "Give, and it shall be given unto you; good measure, pressed down, and shaken together, and running over, shall men give into your bosom. For with the same measure that you portion withal it shall be measured to you again" (Luke 6:38).

Pure vision is a blessing to God and to the people. Never take the approach a pastor did when asked to work on a joint project with other local pastors. He responded with the question: "What's in it for me?" That kind of attitude taints the pure vision of Kingdom mindset for a community. When pastors respect other pastors and churches in a community, the heart of God is revealed in pure vision.

Leaders must keep an open ear to people who love them. A canary in the coal mine can be annoying at times, but if it quits chirping it is dead because of the poisonous gas in the mine. If people quit talking to you and giving their prayerful opinions, it can be deadly for you. Highly critical people can wear you out but don't close off everyone. Your spouse and staff dearly love you. Listen to them. Ask them what they see in you or the way you handle matters in the church and in your personal life. My wife is gifted with wisdom and good common sense. She is not bashful about sharing her opinions. What makes her so easy to listen to is that she always speaks with love and concern. Speaking the truth in love makes it easy to receive. Don't be a know-it-all. Listen to people who love you enough to step out of their comfort zone and speak the truth.

Let's look at David again. We studied how God looked at him, now let's look at what people thought about him. David had seven brothers. When the prophet Samuel came to David's father, Jesse, he didn't mention he had an eighth son. You talk about feeling insignificant. When your own father doesn't see any potential in you, it can take a huge bite out of your confidence. But when Samuel looked at David's seven brothers, he knew the chosen king of Israel was not in that group of young men. So he asked Jesse if he had any more sons. Jesse replied, "One more young boy in the field taking care of the sheep." Samuel requested that David be brought to him while he waited patiently.

You see, man looks on the outward appearance, but God looks on the heart. When David arrived, Samuel knew by the Holy Spirit that David would be the next king of Israel. Samuel anointed him with oil, revealing God's intent. David could have swollen up with pride, but he did just the opposite. He went back to work taking care of his father's sheep. He could have gone to his father with valid complaints, but David put his faith and trust in the Lord to fight his battles. He stayed focused on his job at hand and guarded his heart against any resentment toward his father and brothers.

Don't allow someone else to define you. Your affirmation comes from your Heavenly Father. He sees your pure heart when others see a little boy. Psalm 51:10 gives us the prayer we need: "Create in me a clean heart, O' God." Let my heart be pure in Your eyes that You may be glorified with pure vision.

GOD PREPARES THE VISIONARY

CHAPTER THREE

For every vision, God has a visionary handpicked. He is in no hurry. God is patient and has a plan to take weak, flawed vessels and make them into vessels of honor that will represent Him in the vision. Before the foundations of the world, our names were written in the Lamb's Book of Life (see Daniel 12:1 or Revelation 21:27). He knew before we were born that we would follow Him. He never hurries us into the vision. Everything is strategically planned out in the development of His visionary. He starts when we are young. Long before we know Him, He is developing and molding important traits in us. Long before God was able to start working on my character, He began weaving a good work ethic in me.

I loved the farm life. There was always something to do on the farm. Building fences, cleaning out the barn, milking the cows, feeding the chickens, hogs, and cattle, the work never ceased. Summer was busy planting and working in the garden, thus never a dull moment. I lived for every other day because my brother and I alternated days of driving the tractor. It was like heaven while running the tractor or any type of machinery.

The Lord was preparing me for ministry as a young boy. Any vision worth fulfilling is worthy of hard work. God put

Adam in the Garden of Eden and gave him a purpose - till the garden, which is hard work. Many people have dreams of fulfilling a great vision, but they lack a work ethic. A good work ethic implies the age-old saying, "If you're going to do something, do it right." Colossians 3:23 expands this, "And whatsoever ye do, do it heartily as unto the Lord, and not unto men." The Amplified Bible adds, "...put in your very best effort, as something done for the Lord."

Whatever we do for the Lord, we should do it with excellence. Leith Anderson says, "The same holds true for visionaries. There are certain things that we must do, whether we are experts at them or not, or whether or not we like them."[9]

It is amazing what God can do through us when we are willing to do whatever it takes. The Lord takes broken, flawed people, even those whom the world has given up on, and makes them into vessels of honor. God is so amazingly patient with us. When I couldn't see any signs of a future or anything good in me, He came to me!

GOD IS DRAWN TO THE BROKEN

God sees the potential in everybody. Our Father is the potter and we are the clay (see Isaiah 64:8). In Psalm 51:17 (NLT), we are told God will not reject the broken: "The sacrifice you desire is a broken spirit. You will not reject a broken and repentant heart, O' God." I'm so glad He doesn't throw the clay away. He takes the broken pieces of our lives and puts them back together. When he gets done, we are better than new.

"Therefore, if any man be in Christ, he is a new creature: old things have passed away; behold all things are become new" (2 Corinthians 5:17). Our spirit man is born again, but our soul is a work in progress. Instantly, our soul is improved because of the Lord's presence in our lives. Our mind is renewed by the Word of God. True repentance means we change the way we act and think. God's peace floods our emotions that have been tormented by guilt and shame. Our will is submitted to the Lordship of Jesus. Now, the journey of growing and maturing is a life destined to be conformed to the image of Jesus (see Romans 8:29). This is a lifelong journey. Only the Lord knows when we are ready to be the visionary. I told the Lord when I was a young Christian preparing for my ministry appointment, only You know when I am ready. Much growing and maturing was necessary before I was confident enough to take that step.

Matthew 12:20 is rich with a revelation of the heart of God for the bruised and broken. "He will not crush the weakest reed or put out a flickering candle. Finally, He will cause justice to be victorious" (NLT). The Passion Translation says, "He will be gentle with the weak and feeble". The truth is, when we acknowledge our weaknesses, then we discover His strength. 2 Corinthians 12:9 adds: "And He said unto me, My grace is sufficient for thee: for My strength is made perfect in weaknesses." I am weak, but He is strong. Learning to lean on Jesus is the key to victorious Christian living.

My journey in God's training as a visionary started as a baby Christian. God put a hunger and thirst in my heart for His Word of truth. Reading was a struggle when I got saved, so the Lord really helped me to become a good reader. The Bible became my passion so much that I actually neglected my family. Pat, my wife, said "Steve, the bars used to have my husband, now the Bible has my husband." I apologized to her and tried to balance my Bible reading around family time. I am still in love with God's Word and remain passionate about learning more and more. We should always have a teachable spirit. Never lose the hunger for God's Word. Our family worshiped for ten years at Trinity Full Gospel Church in Zanesville, Ohio. Trinity's Pastor Arnold was a Bible scholar. He and Joyce McNerney taught Bible college on Monday and Tuesday evenings. So, you guessed it, I enrolled in Bible college along with Sunday School and anything else to gain knowledge. I was like a sponge soaking up God's Word.

It is not enough to just gain head knowledge; that only makes one religious like the Pharisees. The Word of God transforms us by the power of the Holy Spirit when we apply it to our lives. Along with receiving God's Word, we also found avenues to proclaim it. After being saved just a few months, the Sunday School superintendent asked me to teach a teens Sunday School class. On my first Sunday, I wanted to run. God helped me stay, and much to my surprise, the teens came back the next week. Shocked, but glad they were hungry for truth, teens would be my ministry for the next five years. When you show a teenager you love them and really care about them, you make a friend for life. They will never forget what you impart in them. Pat and I also started a Friday night Bible Study at our house. Our little house in Philo was full of people starving for fellowship and eager to grow in their faith. We didn't know much about the Bible, but we trusted God to lead us, and He did.

Church Sunday morning and evening, along with Wednesday night and all of the revival services we could attend, was our life. Pat and I both love to sing so we joined the church choir.

There went our Thursday evenings, too. We loved it and wouldn't trade those days for anything. We realized we were being trained and schooled for a higher calling. We had no idea what that calling was, but we were enjoying the journey and getting valuable on-the-job training.

PREPARATION AT A STEEL MILL

How could God use a steel mill job to prepare anybody for ministry? I worked at the Ohio Ferro Alloy in Philo, Ohio for five years. During that time, I was very much unsaved and as wicked as they came. Read my book, *God Has a Man*, for details. Like Paul the Apostle, I was the chiefest of sinners. It was time to go back to work with 600 men most of whom lived just like I had lived. Love and care prompted me to pray for them because I knew what they were going through with their addictions. Many had marriage problems due to their lifestyle. Every day, I would ask the Lord to lead me to somebody who needed to hear about Jesus. The first six months were plowing and planting time. Some co-workers were very hard to reach while others seemed to appreciate the caring witness. All had a wait-and-see attitude. Not one thought I would follow through with my walk of faith which was understandable. It was going to take time. Only with God's grace was I able to keep praying, keep witnessing, and keep clean. Then the first one got saved and then another and another. Eventually, there were 12 men and their families attending our church and Bible study. There was revival in the steel mill and in our church. Little did I know this was part of my training as a visionary.

God wants to save everybody, He just needs somebody to believe and let their light shine so others can see the way. We had just finished the Christmas season. You know what happens next: take down the Christmas tree and decorations. It was time to carry the boxes of decorations down to the basement, and like a typical man, I didn't turn the light on in the storage room. I made it without stumbling and falling. On the way back out of the dark room, I looked down the hallway and there was a dim light at the end of the hallway. I was thinking it would be easy to get out because of the light ahead. That's exactly what people need in order to walk out of darkness. They just need somebody to let their light shine. People are drawn to Jesus through prayer and Christ-filled believers. "We are in training for reigning."[10] When the Spirit of God came on him, David, confronted by the lion or bear, slew them with his bare hands. He did that to protect the sheep. You must love sheep to be willing to jeopardize your life for them. He was in training to be a king who would love God's people one day. God is molding our hearts so we too will love people enough to risk our lives and give our lives to be God's visionary.

PREPARATION ISN'T EASY

People are always looking for the easy way; it is human nature, but it's not God's way. You see, the manger and the cross were not easy for Jesus. He was born into poverty. No crib just a feeding trough to lay Him in as a newborn child. Herrod tried to kill Him when He was about two years old. Jesus was living with parents who, although they knew of His miraculous origins, didn't understand that He was just doing His Father's business. His own brothers and sisters thought He was a lunatic. "He came unto His own, and His own received Him not" (John 1:11).

He was lied about, mocked, spit on, beaten, and nailed to a cross - a criminal's place of punishment. Hebrews 5:8 states, "Though He were a son, yet learned He obedience by the things which He suffered." Through all of this, Jesus prayed not My will be done but Thy will be done. Many people have a misconception of a "vision" and a "visionary." I love the quote "An idea emerges from a self-established call to ministry; a vision emerges from prayer."[11] Jesus' life is marked by continuous prayer. Learn to pray and surrender your will to the Lord, even when you have been wronged.

Years ago, I went through one of the most difficult times in my life of ministry. A Judas betrayed me. He went for the kill. He tried to destroy me. Like Jesus, I had done nothing but good. I had stuck out my neck for this brother. It was grievous, to say the least. For three months I would lie awake at night with nerves in my stomach twitching. Some call them butterflies, mine were more like vultures. Here's the amazing thing; as my betrayer walked out of my office door, the Lord spoke so gently to me, "This is Me." These words gave me great comfort. After searching my heart to see if this was chastising from the Lord for the wrong I had done or an attack from the enemy, still these words came to me, "This is Me." Having placed this entire situation in the Lord's hands, peace came. I chose to forgive this brother. Forgiveness would be necessary many times a day. The Lord did a great work in my heart adding more grace for the hurting. I have thanked the Lord many times for that experience. There was a cleansing of the atmosphere by the presence of the Lord. Though the whole church felt the pain at first, they also felt an air of refreshing and expectation that had moved in. The church has since been on a steady increase spiritually as well as numerically. All eyes were on me during that difficult season. People follow their leader if they believe in him or her. A wise man once said, "I have never seen strong values come out of a committee. Values to be held passionately, require a point person."[12]

JOSEPH'S STORY

We all love the story of Joseph, but none of us want to walk in his steps. Joseph had it made by being his father's favorite son. Though he was the eleventh son, his father Jacob gave him the coat of many colors. It was a mark of honor and rank worn only by the chief heir. Joseph inherited the birthright which was designated to the firstborn (see Genesis 37:3). The Lord gave Joseph two dreams, and both were interpreted that his brothers and father would bow down and give him homage. Joseph was very loyal to his father and would report to him the wrongs his brothers were doing. Thus, Joseph's brothers hated him with a passion. It's important to learn not to share everything the Lord shows you with others. Pray and ask the Lord what to do with your dream or vision. Sometimes your greatest gift can become your greatest weakness. Eventually, Joseph's brothers planned to kill him and throw him into a pit. His brother Reuben stopped them from killing him and instead took his coat and threw him in a pit (see Genesis 37:24).

At that time, Ishmaelite traders were traveling by, so the brothers decided to sell Joseph into slavery. When they arrived in Egypt, they sold him to Potiphar, an officer of Pharaoh. In Genesis 39:2, Joseph is favored by the Lord at Potiphar's house. He is made head of the house, and all is well until Potiphar's wife makes advances to Joseph. When he rejects her, refusing to sin against his God, she lies to her husband and accuses Joseph of attempted rape. Joseph is cast into prison but again, the Lord prospers him (see Genesis 39:23). He was made the chief warden over all the prisoners. Several years passed and Pharaoh had two troubling dreams that no one could interpret. At that time, the chief butler remembered that Joseph had interpreted a dream for him when he was in prison. Joseph was brought before Pharaoh, and he interpreted both dreams as one. The dreams revealed there would be seven prosperous years coming and then seven years of famine. Pharaoh knew this was correct and elevated Joseph to the second highest position in all of Egypt.

Now when the famine was felt by Joseph's father Jacob, and his family, he sent some of his sons to Egypt to buy food. Jacob believed Joseph was dead, and Joseph's brothers thought he was likely dead or a slave someplace in Egypt. They didn't have a clue that Joseph was the one they would face when they arrived. In Genesis 50:17-21, Joseph reveals to his brothers his identity. They feared for their lives. Joseph wept while his brothers fell at his feet and vowed to serve him. He told them to fear not, and he comforted them and promised to take care of them and their families. Then he revealed God's plan. "You thought evil against me, but God meant it unto good" (Genesis 50:20). Joseph's father and 70 family members journeyed to Egypt, and their lives were preserved because of God's plan and His visionary-in-training.

Here is a beautiful truth: man can strip you of your favor, but God will give it back multiplied many times over. The key result was that Joseph never became bitter, only better. I'm convinced you can trust God no matter what you are going through. God is preparing His visionary.

ADVERSITY UNIVERSITY

In the School of Ministry, Mark Pfeifer teaches about *WAIT*. The acronym stands for *Word, Adversity, Isolation,* and *Time*.[13] While waiting on our assignment we will be enrolled in Adversity University. It is God who enrolls us. Our flesh pulls away from any type of adversity.

The *Word* of God is our change agent: "For the Word of God is quick, and powerful, and sharper than any two-edged sword, piercing even to the dividing asunder of soul and spirit, and of the joints and marrow, and is a discerner of the thoughts and intents of the heart" (Hebrews 4:12). What does this change look like? "But Jesus answered and said, 'It is written, Man shall not live by bread alone, but by every word that proceedeth out of the mouth of God" (Matthew 4:4).

Adversity or resistance builds our spiritual muscles. It drives us closer to the Lord and makes us dependent on Him.

Isolation must be directed by the Lord. For example, when Moses, went up on Mt. Sinai alone and communed with the Lord.

At that *Time* God gave Moses the law for Israel to live by. In times of isolation, the Lord speaks to His servant and gives direction and instruction. Timing is everything in God's kingdom. In God's perfect timing, all the pieces of the puzzle fall into place. The ancient Greek word Kairos means time, but not just any time. Kairos is about timeliness: the special moment when it's the opportune time to say or do a particular thing. If things aren't coming together, wait for that Kairos time. In God's time, all things work together for good for those who love God and are called according to His purpose (see Romans 8:28). In your time of *WAIT*, be determined to walk it through. Like Jimmy Valvano said in his speech shortly before he died of cancer, "Don't give up, don't ever give up."[14]

THE IBERVILLEA SONORAE

I have always loved and admired nature, it is God's amazing creation. For example, His concept of waiting is well illustrated by the Ibervillea Sonorae plant. It can survive for seven years without soil or water; while living in adversity and isolation. The persistence of that little plant is amazing. Yet, even it will eventually fade and die. Don't camp in *WAIT* forever. Know when your training is complete and enjoy graduation time. "They that wait upon the Lord shall renew their strength; they shall mount up with wings as eagles; they shall run and not be weary; and they shall walk and not faint" (Isaiah 40:31).

THE HOLY SPIRIT

My wife and I were saved in a Nazarene Church in Chesterhill, Ohio. We are grateful for a church that preached salvation. However, while reading the Bible concerning the Holy Spirit baptism, I discovered my church believed that to speak in tongues or to seek to speak in tongues was an unclean spirit or of the devil. In Acts 2:4, believers were filled with the Holy Ghost and spoke in other tongues. "For they have heard them speak with tongues and magnify God" (Acts 10:46). Also in Acts 19:6, "And when Paul laid his hands upon them, the Holy Ghost came on them; and they spake with tongues and prophesied." Conversely, I don't believe that you must speak with tongues to be saved. Salvation comes when we believe in Jesus Christ and confess Him as our Savior (see Romans 10:9-10).

However, as a young believer, I desired everything God had for me, even the baptism of the Holy Ghost. I knew that the Holy Spirit dwelt within me at conversion because of Titus 3:5, "Not by works of righteousness which we have done, but according to His mercy He saved us, by the washing of regeneration, and renewing of the Holy Ghost" and Acts 1:8: "But ye shall receive power, after that the Holy Ghost is come upon you: and ye shall be witnesses unto me." I needed that power within me in order to be a victorious, overcoming believer. The Greek word for power is Dunamis - ability, power. I began to read every scripture pertaining to the baptism of the Holy Spirit. I started seeking the gift but struggled to receive it, not realizing anything that is received by God is by faith. Quoting scripture to God that He already knew didn't work. The promise was mine, yet I did not realize how to receive it by faith.

By this time, we had been led by the Lord to a Spirit-filled church in Zanesville. Our assistant pastor visited us at our home one evening. He was so full of the Spirit and explained that God wanted to fill every believer with the Holy Spirit. When he left that night, I knew it was my time to receive. The Lord seemed to say to me, I want you to have the baptism of the Holy Spirit more than you want it. Pat went to bed and I stayed up to receive the baptism of the Spirit. She said "Is it okay if I go to bed?", but later told me that when she lay down she felt a strong presence of the Holy Spirit. Kneeling at the couch in the living room, I prayed, "Lord Jesus, fill me with the Holy Ghost." Instantly, a thought entered my mind - not tonight, it's too late. Realizing that was not the Lord's thought, I began praising Jesus for all He had done for me. The Holy Spirit walked into our house through the kitchen. My hands began to turn numb similar to the feeling of Novocaine that a dentist would use when filling a tooth. That presence of the Holy Spirit flowed down my arms and face at the same time. When the power sensation reached my stomach, my language began to change to a language I'd never spoken. Joy flooded my entire being. I laughed and cried, and then laughed and cried some more. Then both of my hands were cramped with excruciating pain as if nails were being driven through them. Praying, "Lord, I can't stand this!" He replied, "Just think of what my Son went through on the cross." The pain left but weeping continued as I gave praise to God. This experience lasted for about 45 minutes. The thought of having a million dollars or this precious gift entered my mind. Burn the money and keeping the precious gift just received was an easy choice.

As my faith and understanding of the communion with the Holy Spirit grew, I learned to listen to Him: "For as many as are led by the Spirit of God, they are the sons of God" (Romans 8:14). We understand as sons of God the Holy Spirit wants to lead and order our every step and every decision. He will guide us into all truth (see John 16:13). The Holy Spirit began to increase His anointing in my life and ministry. I realized God was preparing me to be a visionary, and the Holy Spirit was the one who was orchestrating the preparation process. This precious anointing of the Holy Spirit destroys every yoke of the enemy. The Holy Spirit will destroy every hindrance and teach you all things you need to know. He is the great Teacher.

SOME THINGS NEVER CHANGE

God's preparation for Moses to become a visionary leader took 40 years. Moses supposed the time was right when he was 40 years old. He defended a Hebrew brother who was mistreated by an Egyptian soldier. The word got out that he had killed an Egyptian and he had to flee for his life to Midian. There he tended sheep for the next 40 years. He went from the palace life where he was raised, to the rough desert life. It was a humbling experience for Moses, but God used it to prepare him for the great task of delivering the Hebrews from Egyptian bondage (see Acts 7:22-25).

I was a young minister working as an assistant pastor, burning the candle at both ends for a long time. I was trying to win the world to Jesus all by myself. On the brink of burnout, I had a life-changing experience. While cutting firewood on a ladder, the limb I was cutting swung back and knocked the ladder out from under me. Not too smart. The ladder, limb, chainsaw, and I all hit the ground. I tried to stand up but quickly realized my leg was injured. While waiting for the emergency squad to arrive, my prayer was, "Lord, let me be injured enough so I won't have to go to church tomorrow." It was a tell-tale sign of burnout. I spent a few weeks in bed and on an immobilizer for a month. During that time praying and reading my Bible were my two pastimes. One day I went outside and laid under the shade tree on a blanket to read my Bible. Pat asked, "Do you know how long it's been since you've done this?" That accident may have saved my spiritual life. I was restored physically and spiritually by the Lord during that time. Like Moses, we need time to reflect and allow the Lord to teach us some valuable lessons of life and ministry. God is preparing you every day of your life to be a visionary.

VISION WITH STRATEGY

CHAPTER FOUR

An elderly lady in Africa was born blind. She wanted to reach school students with the gospel, so she came up with a plan. She'd give each student a Bible and then have them read a highlighted verse: John 3:16. She led many students to the Lord and twenty-four of them became pastors. This woman didn't look at her limitations, she developed a strategy. Everything a person does requires a strategy. Webster's Dictionary defines strategy as: "a plan or a method." I heard a quote years ago, "Plan your work and work your plan."

My wife and I have a small farm of about sixty acres. It's a hobby farm, something I am passionate about. Pat said years ago that she had never seen me happier than now, living on a farm. Having been raised on a farm it seems to get in your blood. There are so many life lessons to be learned on the farm. The greatest lesson is having a strategy. Every day you have work to do: feeding the cattle, cleaning out the barn, checking the water supply, counting the herd, and watching for any signs of sickness. The work is never done. If you're going to have animals, you're going to have responsibility. With responsibility, there must be a strategy. When we bought the farm there was no fence, no barn, or house. The plan was to build a house for us to live in, and then we would build the barn and a detached garage. Poor planning - we built them all in one summer. Jamie, our son, and a lot of friends helped us. We also built a fence around the 40 acres of farmable land. All that building required strategy and planning. A man will lay in bed at night rehashing his day of accomplishments and planning the next step for tomorrow's project. Life requires a strategy. The person without a plan for their life is like a blind man without a friend to guide him. Ministry or pastoring a church without a plan will go nowhere. If something is worth doing, it deserves a plan.

STRATEGY OR FANTASY?

The difference between having a fantasy and a vision is finding a strategy. Many people have fantasies. They can dream up all kinds of stuff about how great their lives and ministries will be someday. The problem is it will never happen. Why? Without a strategy, a vision is simply a fantasy. Not only does God want to give his people a fantastic vision of what can be achieved (a picture of the end result), but He also wants to graciously give us a strategy on how to get there. Examples:

- God gave Adam a vision for dominion and a strategy to get there.
- God gave Noah a vision for survival and a strategy to get there.
- God gave Abraham a vision for a biblical nation and a strategy to get there.
- God gave Moses a vision of how the nation's

government should function and a strategy to get there.

- God gave Joshua a vision for victory and a strategy to get there.
- God gave David a vision for a throne and a strategy to get there.
- Jesus gave His disciples a vision for reaching the nations of the earth and a strategy to get there in His Mount of Olives sermon.

Everybody has problems! People see problems. Visionaries see answers. Strategists see how to get there. What I am suggesting is that we become more than leaders who talk about the problems in our churches and more than leaders who talk about where we want our churches to go. I am praying that God gives us a strategy for how to get there. This will separate the dreamers from the achievers. I want to experience the vision and not just talk about it.

THE WATERSHED OF THE MUSKINGUM

In the early 1990's the Lord dropped into my spirit the desire to begin praying for the Watershed of the Muskingum. Specifically, to pray that God would bring revival. We made large poster-sized maps of the State of Ohio and highlighted the Watershed of Muskingum which occupies about one-fifth of the state. The posters were put in our church members' prayer rooms, homes, and offices to remind us to pray for revival. I told a guest minister that we were believing for revival. He said, "How are you going to do that?" I immediately responded; God will show us. For over twenty-five years we have continued to pray for revival and for the people of the Watershed area to be saved. I didn't have a strategy, but God did.

In August of 2021, a friend and I were meeting for lunch. Gary had recently begun attending Cornerstone Church, and we seemed to be developing a strong friendship orchestrated by the Lord. I had plans to introduce a new ministry to him called LifeWise Academy. Before I could inject my thoughts, Gary asked, "Have you ever heard about LifeWise Academy?" I replied, "I was going to ask you the same question." LifeWise is very new, but the Supreme Court ruled in 1952 that a program like this could function. It is called Release Time for Religious Instruction (RTRI). Although legal for decades, RTRI has been almost completely unknown by the Christian Church. The Case of Zorach vs. Clauson was ruled as constitutional by the Supreme Court making it legal to teach religious instruction to public school students during school hours. The requirements are that it must be privately funded, held off school property, and parentally approved. We discussed that day over lunch how to start a LifeWise Academy program in our school district. That day we committed ourselves and our resources to the project and began working on a strategy. By the fall of 2022, Franklin Local Schools LifeWise Academy was up and running in grades Kindergarten through Fourth. By the beginning of the next school year, we had expanded to include grades Five and Six. The Lord has used Gary Phipps to share LifeWise with the school districts of Muskingum

County, surrounding counties, and even states as far away as Florida. LifeWise began operations in 2019 and now has opened academies in 700 school districts. I see this as a part of God's plan to win, not only the Watershed of Muskingum, but also to bring revival to our nation. This is a movement sweeping our country. To God be the glory. LifeWise is a gift from God. It's amazing that He opened the door in 1952 and we are just now stepping through it. The Lord's patience with us is truly of biblical proportions.

The Lord of the harvest is sending laborers for the harvest. God has a plan and strategy for the Watershed of the Muskingum. It's a plan to win souls into God's kingdom.

CROSSING THE JORDAN STRATEGY

The historic stories of the Old Testament never grow old. When Israel crossed the Jordan River on dry ground it was a result of the priests' obedience to the Lord's command. The priests were instructed to pick up the Ark of the Covenant and carry it into the raging Jordan River. Leadership is to carry the Presence of God everywhere they go. His Presence is always first. The Lord instructed the people to put a space of four-fifths of a mile between the Ark and the people. He wanted everybody to see the miracle He performed. They were told to walk into a raging river with God's Ark in the hands of the priests. As their feet pierced the water, God backed the water up to the city of Adam. This was God's strategy for Israel to enter the Promised Land. God's strategies may not always seem to us to be realistic. This would build the faith of all the Israelites as they followed the Lord's perfect strategy (see Joshua 3:3-16).

UNLIMITED VISION

God's vision is truly unlimited. There is no problem too big that the Lord does not have an answer for. "Now unto Him that is able to do exceedingly abundantly above all that we ask or think" (Ephesians 3:20). If God would give such unlimited vision and strategy to Abraham that Sarah (who was barren and ninety years old) would have a son of promise, what can He do through you and me? Just like God chose to work through Abraham based on his obedience, if we are obedient, we qualify for God to use us. God gives our minds visions of His plan. Great blessings follow what we see by the Spirit.

STRATEGY FOR DISCIPLESHIP

Most churches' schedules are full year-round. Sometimes we find ourselves busy but not accomplishing much in the Kingdom of God. We might have conferences, revivals, and teaching emphasis but miss the mark of a holistic model for making disciples. Jesus told us in Matthew 28:19, "Go ye therefore, and teach all nations, baptizing them in the name of the Father, and of the Son, and of the Holy Ghost." It is not enough just to win souls. That soul must be taught the Word and modeled into Christ's likeness. To win a soul and not disciple them is as deadly as giving birth to a baby and laying it on the front porch and saying have a good life. Every church needs a well-designed strategy for discipling newborn Christians through to maturity. Cornerstone Church has been working to perfect this strategy for 38 years. We have never thought this is good enough; we are always looking for and praying about new ideas and methods for discipleship.

Over the years we have developed numerous discipleship courses. They all had their time and season. We combined the best of all the courses and produced what we call Foundations for Life (FFL). You can have the best teaching material but if you don't have a gifted teacher, the Word will not come alive to the hearer. We have been blessed with one of the most passionate, gifted teachers that I know, Darla Wahl. FFL lays a good foundation of the Word of God in the hearts of the students. We start with the basics of the Salvation Plan and finish with how to serve the Lord in church and community.

The following is the *Foundations for Life Course* outline given to each participant:[15]

LESSON ONE – UNDERSTAND YOUR NEW LIFE
This lesson takes you through your connection to God and the local church body. We'll discuss where you came from, where you are now, and where you are going.

LESSON TWO – OVERCOMING SIN
Sin separates us from God. This lesson will address what sin is, how it can affect us, and how God handles sin. We will walk through God's plan to redeem us and how repentance can lead us back to fellowship with God.

LESSON THREE – THE VICTORY OF FAITH THROUGH GOD'S WORD

The Word of God is life-giving. In this lesson, we'll talk about the importance of God's Word and how to rely on the Holy Spirit to teach us the Word. Our faith, what it means, and how we can increase it, will also be explored.

LESSON FOUR – THE POWER OF PRAYER

In Lesson Four we cover prayer and how it ties in with our faith. Through prayer, we can draw near to God. We'll discuss how to pray effectively and learn how to recognize hindrances to prayer.

LESSON FIVE – KNOWING JESUS

In lesson five we will discuss who Jesus is and look at His humanity as well as His mission here on earth. Through His death and resurrection, we can better understand His victory over death and look forward to His second coming.

LESSON SIX – VESSELS READY FOR HIS SERVICE

God has given us authority, but it requires proper order and function. In Lesson Six, we will discuss how to function within that God-given authority to lead an effective and faithful ministry here on earth.

A MOVING TARGET

Over the years I came to realize that Cornerstone Church is a moving target. If you don't like change, you won't like Cornerstone Church. No ministry is perfect and needs to be tweaked a little from time-to-time. Usually, it requires just a little adjustment, but sometimes you have to scrap something and start over again. We, like so many churches, have found it necessary to adjust how we do church services. For years we would average several hundred people on a Sunday evening service and a good attendance on Wednesday evening. Due to a cultural change in sports activities for children, it has become harder and harder for parents to fit everything into the week's schedule. Sad to say, many chose to delete extra church services to make time for sports and extracurricular activities. The attendance slowly decreased until we realized it was time for change. That's when we began to explore the idea of small groups. We studied many models and attended many "cell" church conferences. We tried to duplicate some of those models but struggled to find our niche.

Finally, we asked the Lord what He wanted our small groups to look like. It's amazing how things come together when you give Him the reigns.

We have discovered that small groups are a very effective strategy for discipling believers. At Cornerstone Church, we call them C-12 Groups. The "C" stands for connecting and the "12" stands for discipling. This format gives people an avenue for fellowship and Bible study. People are able to share testimonies, ask questions, and pray for each other. These groups are a place where life is experienced. It is a conducive atmosphere for the gifts of the Spirit as well. People build lifelong relationships and become family in small groups. I call fellowship a little taste of heaven on earth. This concept is very much scriptural.

- "And they, continuing daily with one accord in the temple, and breaking bread from house to house, did eat their meat with gladness and singleness of heart" (Acts 2:46).
- "And daily in the temple and in every house, they ceased not to teach and preach Jesus Christ" (Acts 5:42).
- In Acts 20:20, Paul taught believers by going from house to house.

We have discovered that no matter where believers gather, the Lord is there, and people are blessed: "And, lo, I am with you always, even unto the end of the world. Amen" (Matthew 28:20b). Our C-12 groups are diverse in meeting places and style. Groups meet every day of the week at the church, Barracks Youth Center, various homes, the Shelter House, and even in restaurants. Nobody ever has to be lonely or bored. The groups vary from Bible study to pickleball with devotions, disc golf with devotions, Bible study and a meal, widows' group, lunch with the guys, ladies' tea, and even devotions with an exercise class. It is a joy to see people connect, have fun, and grow in their faith. We encourage every member to be a part of a C-12 group. Some attend more than one. I love it! During one of our Foundations for Life classes, our C-12 leaders are invited to present to the class information about their group. Our C-12 leaders are also encouraged to mingle before and after church services to get to know people and invite them to their groups. People need to be wanted, needed, and loved.

We have steadily grown over the past few years, and will soon double the number of our C-12 groups. We came to realize that until you have good solid leadership it is best to wait and be patient. Everything rises or falls on leadership.

CHURCH STRATEGY

There are many models for church planting. When we pioneered Cornerstone Church, we had no model except the Bible. People asked me, "What are we going to do concerning a constitution and by-laws?" I was able to put their minds at ease after talking to Dr. Charles Travis. He informed me that we had a whole year to establish those documents. I knew what to do on Sunday: preach the Word, worship the Lord, pray, and encourage the people. Having been an assistant pastor for five years, I knew how to visit and pray for people. Counseling seemed to come naturally. Sharing God's Word with people concerning their needs and problems worked miracles in their lives. For the administrative aspect of ministry, I was able to lean on Charlie McCloud, one of the founding elders and a very successful businessman. That he was my best friend and a hard worker was a big help. So, we learned a lot by trial and error. How true it is, "You're going to make mistakes, just avoid making big mistakes." Big mistakes hurt a lot of people. It's like throwing a pebble into a pond, it makes little waves. If you throw a boulder into a pond, it makes big waves. People will let you make little mistakes if you take ownership of them and learn from them. Big mistakes hurt a lot of people and can set the ministry back for years.

CHANGE

Anything that grows takes on change or it dies. My friend, Mark Pfeifer, has some good insight on change,

> "The new things of God demand change. Most people don't like to change. Why? Change can be challenging and takes one out of their comfort zone. Some people want to change all the time for no apparent reason. The answer is to be willing to change for the sake of creating positive change. God's first revelation to Joshua was 'Moses is dead' (Joshua 1:1-2). Joshua was forced into change, Moses was gone, and now he is the leader. All eyes were upon him. He would be the catalyst for change for three million Israelites. He would be forced to direct change from being nomads to warriors. As nomads their priorities were carrying water, pitching tents, and valuing their shoes. Now as warriors their priorities would shift to carrying weapons, making fortresses, and valuing their swords. When Joshua took over as their leader Israel was at the Jordan River preparing to cross into the Canaan Land. The river was at flood stage. God brought them

to the Jordan at this time and parted the waters so they could walk over on dry ground. Why during flood time, you might ask? So, Israel couldn't cross back into the wilderness. The Israelites were notorious for wanting to go back to Egypt. The Lord set a roadblock so they couldn't change their minds and return. Movement and life create change. Always ask yourself, is this a necessary or novel change? Change is necessary when growth demands it."[16]

It's like when your child grows out of his size 5 shoe. He might say, "I love my Jordan Airs," but Mom realizes if she doesn't require him to change to size 6, his feet could be damaged or even left crippled. Changing shoe size is necessary! Novel change is changing just for the sake of change and is not healthy. Try to get people to change the pew they sit in for no reason. You get resistance! Learn to embrace change, when it is necessary, on God's timetable.

The bottom line in strategy is knowing the plan that will take you from where you are to where God wants you to be and then fulfilling the task God has for you to achieve. A card player can have the best hand, but if he doesn't know strategy, he can still lose the game. A mountain climber might have the best equipment money can buy, but if he doesn't know the strategy, he might fall to his or her death. A preacher can have great knowledge of the Bible, but if he or she does not have a strategy from heaven, it will be of little benefit to the hearer. You can have the best facilities a Church would want to have, but without a strategy, the church will never fulfill the vision

God has planned for that house.

With every vision comes God's strategy. He always requires us to seek him to turn every page of the strategy manual. When each page is clear, and we obey his plan, the Kingdom of God is advanced! When God's Kingdom is established in a place, lives and communities are transformed. As a computer downloads information that you are seeking, so the Lord of heaven downloads strategy to the earnest seeker! The Lord gives us creative strategies to fulfill His vision. That strategy is His plan for who is to be our mate, where we are to live, and where we are to serve Him in whatever capacity of ministry He has called us to, "Commit thy works unto the Lord, and thy thoughts shall be established" (Proverbs 16:3). Don't grasp at straws, let God direct your every thought. Walk out your vision with God's strategy allowing Him to order your every thought and decision. He is the wise Strategist.

In contrast, God's strategy is not available to secular society: "But the natural man receiveth not the things of the Spirit of God: for they are foolishness onto him: neither can he know them, because they are spiritually discerned" (1 Corinthians 2:14).

VISION AND FAITH

CHAPTER FIVE

Vision is a wonderful gift from God, but without faith it goes nowhere. Faith is the fuel that feeds and propels the vision. Faith and vision go hand in hand. God will never give you a vision without giving you faith to drive the vision: "...according as God hath dealt to every man the measure of faith" (Romans 12:3b). In Greek, a measure is a metron, which means a portion. God has given us a portion of His faith. The same faith that God operates with, that created all things, He has given to us a portion of it (see Hebrews 11:3). The possibilities are limitless when we learn to operate in faith. Faith is given to us in seed form. As we water and feed our faith it grows. It has been said, feed your faith and starve your doubts to death. The Word of God is faith food, "So then faith cometh by hearing and by hearing the Word of God" (Romans 10:17). Read it, believe it, speak it, and watch your faith grow in leaps and bounds.

MY FAITH JOURNEY

It is amazing how God will take a person with no faith, plant a seed of faith in that person, and it begins to grow. I was that person, shifting from a life of trusting in myself to trusting in God. Instantly, life became much easier in this faith walk. I was fascinated with the subject of faith. You could find me reading everything available about faith and even asking God for the gift of faith, not even knowing what it was. My goal was to develop my faith into a mountain-moving faith. We must realize the importance of consistency in our language of faith. Some people talk of faith and doubt in the same sentence. It doesn't work that way. You either trust God or you don't.

As my faith grew, God gave me opportunities to use it. I was once in the hospital for three days with kidney stones. The pain was excruciating, requiring shots for pain every four hours. A Christian friend came to visit me, and he brought me the book: Ever Increasing Faith. Reading the first few pages of the book, the Lord asked me what I was doing laying in that bed sick. I replied, "I don't know, You've already paid the price for my healing." Getting out of bed, bent over in pain, I walked to the restroom to pray. My prayer was for the Lord to dissolve my kidney stones in Jesus' name. Having prayed "in Jesus' name" the pain left. My doctor came in to visit me and I told him what had happened. He ordered x-rays and the results came back with no sign of the kidney stones. The doctor scratched his head, turned, and walked out of the room. God was slowly growing my faith. There were many obstacles I would have to overcome through faith.

After working as a Christian for five years at the Ohio Ferro Alloy, the layoff came. Some men were fearful because of the threat of the plant being shut down completely. Knowing God was closing one door for me to open another door, I signed up for unemployment and used the next six months to complete my ministerial studies. At that time, my home church needed an assistant pastor. After much discussion and prayer, the board of the church hired me as a full- time assistant pastor. I was so excited and grateful for the opportunity to serve in my home church. It was a dream come true.

Now my faith would be greatly stretched like never before. Preaching never came easy for me. I struggled with giving a book report in school and this seemed even harder. Having taught the Bible for six years in Sunday school was a great experience, but this was different. With much prayer and learning to trust God with total dependence, I pressed on. The Lord blessed me by continuing to increase His anointing over the years. The anointing makes preaching a delight. Having come to realize that if God can speak through a donkey to Balaam, He can speak through me.

FAITH FOR THE VISION

When the Lord gave me the vision of the church in the cornfield in Duncan Falls, my faith was ready for the task. I knew where the will of God took me, the grace of God would keep me. As the glory of God descended from the heavens and shined on the church building, it spread in all directions. Immediately, I knew this was bigger than me. This was a God-size vision. I shared the vision with my wife, and she never batted an eye. She said, "Steve, you have never led me astray before, and if you say this is God, I am with you." It is imperative that your mate is with you one hundred percent because they can make or break you. A faithful helpmate is worth their weight in gold. Pat has always been supportive and encouraging when I needed a little boost. After announcing what the Lord had shown me and we started a new church in Duncan Falls, people would ask, "Are you afraid? You are leaving a good secure position with no help or backing." I replied, "I would be afraid if I refused to obey God." There was no fear at all, only the faith that God had given me. It was supernatural. God enabled me to look past the natural and see what He was going to do. It was so exciting to think that God would choose to use me for this new church plant.

The first Sunday in May of 1986 we opened the church at the American Legion Hall in Duncan Falls. The building was made of block walls and a concrete floor. It had no air conditioning, but that didn't matter. It was home from the first service. It felt like a family reunion. Everybody was so happy and full of joy. The expectancy level was sky-high, actually, it was more like heaven- high. We praised the Lord, preached the Word, and God moved. One family got saved and our state superintendent's wife testified about receiving healing in her body. We never complained about what we didn't have in material things and buildings. We were so grateful for the vision and the faith to walk it out. Three months later, after much prayer and the grace of God, the Philo High School auditorium became available to rent for Sunday services. This gave us ample room to grow and time to save money to build a church building. The first year we averaged 165 people in attendance at Sunday morning services. The faith and excitement continued to grow. We were excited about what the Lord was doing. People were being saved, families restored, and sick bodies healed. It was a continuous environment of revival. One Sunday morning, near the end of the sermon, I spotted some people from my school days. Wayne & Pat Bassel, and Steve & Vicki Smith were in church with us in the high school auditorium. I nearly fell off the stage with shock. The last time I saw Wayne was at the Alloy. He was driving a truck and stopped for a load of metal. While sharing my faith in Jesus with him, he was not at all impressed. He laughed at me that day. Several years later, at the end of his rope, he cried out to Jesus and was gloriously saved. Little did all of us know that Steve would become my assistant pastor and serve for the next 18 years. We were seeing the fruit of the vision and faith in operation in our very midst.

Two years passed by quickly. The Lord helped us to save $87,000. We were ready to build a church in Duncan Falls, except we hadn't been able to purchase land to build on. My prayer was "Lord, speak to somebody to give us 12 to 15 acres of land." Nobody stepped up to the plate... but God. Pine Knolls Country Club had purchased 152 acres of farmland to develop a golf course. When the local power plant and then the Alloy shut down, Duncan Falls became a depressed area. The plans for a golf course fell through and now the 152-acre farm was for sale. We were able to purchase it with cash. Where God gives vision, He also gives provision. While saving money to build a church, a Doctor from Columbus was in between churches and sent his $2500 monthly tithe to our church. He had been told about the new church plant and wanted to help until he found a church home. Soon we had one testimony after another of the Lord speaking to people to give. When I met with Ron McHenry (a member of our church along with his wife, Bonnie) our general contractor, we drew up a rough sketch of a building. I asked Ron how much this would cost. He replied, "about half a million dollars." I said, "Ron, we're done with the meeting for today." I couldn't wrap my mind around that much money. After a time in prayer, my faith rose to the level of trusting God for the money. Even people at the church struggled to see how we were going to be able to get enough money. Without wavering, I kept speaking faith to the congregation. God owns it all, He owns the cattle on a thousand hilltops and the hills belong to Him, too. After purchasing the land, we were about broke. One month before we were to sign papers at the closing, the vice president of the bank, Mr. French called to tell me the loan was secure, but the board of Century National Bank wanted a $50,000 down payment. I said, ok thanks, and put it in the Lord's hand. Sitting down at the table, the phone rang. It was a local farmer. He asked, "When are you going to sell me that 50 acres of farmland?" I said, "I'll get back with you." That sale was $40,000, and in one month we raised the rest of the down payment.

Another miracle occurred. Six months from the time we broke ground, the church was finished and we moved into a beautiful sanctuary. Ron and his son Keith had worked hard to complete the building in record time. Normally it takes a lot longer than six months to build a house, but when God is in it, miracles take place. The sanctuary seated 500 people with a large balcony, but everything else was too small. The Lord gave us an idea of how to pay the church off in five years. We had 52 acres that bordered the back end of the Pine Knolls Subdivision which was mostly a wooded area. We subdivided it into ten five-acre lots and they sold like hotcakes. Every penny we made we put toward the mortgage. Our secretary, Virginia Thomas, had a plan to put extra envelopes in each pew and to ask people to give at least a dollar or whatever they wanted to put into it weekly. Hundreds of dollars came in weekly. God is good. Even the tellers at the bank were excited to see how much extra money we would bring in weekly. By 1995, we burned the mortgage of the building loan. It was a great milestone and a true testament of what people can do when they work together for a cause. The church had grown to its capacity, and we were in the planning stages of a 1200-seat sanctuary. Phil Johnson, a building contractor, and his wife, Mary Lou, are members of Cornerstone. We gladly hired Phil to be the general contractor. This sanctuary took a little longer to build. After 13 months, in December of 1998, we moved into our new sanctuary. We celebrated for a short time because the first sanctuary had to be remodeled. It was finished with mostly volunteer workers in the church. It took us seven months to complete it, but it was worth it. The new sanctuary cost 1.2 million dollars, but with the Lord's help, it was paid off in about ten years.

One of the greatest blessings to the church and the community has been the Barracks Youth Center. It is used every day of the week. From children playing basketball, archery classes, youth services, Bible studies, pickleball for adults, church dinners, Franklin Local Elementary Schools, birthday parties, and much, much more. It was a vision that Pastor Tim Alexander and Keith Wahl had. About a year after we completed the second sanctuary, Pastor Tim and Keith wanted to talk about a vision they had. Now, I had vowed to build nothing else until the new sanctuary was paid for. Sitting in my office they both began to tell me of their vision of a 120' by 80' youth center. I must admit, I laughed at both of them. They said, we are not talking right now, but in the future. I had to apologize to them for laughing. We started raising the money. Charlie McCloud organized an auction for us and served as auctioneer. We raised $50,000 for the youth center. That year we saved and in a little over a year, we had $260,000 in the bank to build the center. It is truly amazing what you can do if God is in it. Every step is a step of faith with His blessing meeting every need.

When we started the church in 1986, we felt like one day we would have a ministry for unwed mothers. We had no understanding of what that would look like in the future. In 2014, we opened the doors of Naomi House for women struggling with addictions. We began remodeling the facilities for Naomi House in 2013, along with three other buildings to create a Christian Camp. Most of the work was completed by volunteer labor of the people at our church. Naomi House has shifted to a halfway house for women. Another of the Christian camp buildings houses the LifeWise Academy of Franklin Local. Every building the Lord has helped us to build is dedicated to the Lord's work. The Lord has helped us be debt-free for years. To God be the glory. This has allowed us to hire a great staff and be supporters of other ministries locally, nationally, and globally.

THE EYE OF FAITH

Israel had camped by the Jordan River for one year after

crossing the Jordan. Jericho was in sight, but the Lord wanted them to rest for that year before they would begin conquering Canaan land. Additionally, "The Lord said unto Joshua, see I have given into thine hand Jericho, and the king thereof, and the mighty men of valor" (Joshua 6:2). Notice what the Lord said to Joshua, "See I have given Jericho into thine hands." In other words, Joshua, see through the eye of faith that I have given Jericho to you. The visionary sees the vision long before it is a reality. God told Joshua to circle the city once a day for six days. The seven priests were to lead the Ark with trumpets of rams' horns. On the seventh day they were to circle the city seven times. Then the priests were to blow the trumpets with a long blast. The armed men were to go first, then the priests and the rear guard came behind the Ark. The people were not to speak a word while circling the city. After the priests blew the trumpets, the people were to face the city and shout (See Joshua 6). God promised the walls would fall down.

Through the eye of faith, Joshua had already seen the walls fall down flat. As he walked out the Lord's commands, the people were beginning to see the vision as well. The armed men symbolized God's protection before and behind the Ark and the priests. God goes before us, and He has our back too. The people represent the church on the move. The faith walk is a walk of action, victory, and overcoming. Joshua is God's messenger giving the orders of the Lord. The Ark is the Presence of the Lord. Who can stand in the Lord's Presence? No one, for the Lord, is strong and mighty! The priests represent God's authority. The trumpet blast is a powerful dull sound suggesting the power of God. The shout is a shout of expected victory. Why were they to keep silent? When God speaks, keep silent, obey Him, and watch what He will do. If one person had complained about the long distance around Jericho, the sin of doubt could have spread like wildfire. It was a miracle that nobody said a word until the signal to shout.

Imagine circling a walled city, whose walls were thick enough for chariots to run on top of them, all the way around the city. Every Israelite realized this was going to take a miracle. They gave no room for doubt, they kept their eyes on the prize, the promise. They had been taught well.

Joshua and Caleb wholly followed the Lord (see Numbers 32:12). This generation was different from the previous one. The older generation was stiff-necked and rebellious, but the newer generation was strong in faith and willing to follow God's appointed leader.

As Dale Galloway points out: "You need the eye of an eagle to move beyond the maintenance mentality to become a mission that makes a difference in your community by reaching people for Christ."[17] He adds: "Vision provides an energizing force for a congregation even as it produces a picture of a faith-inspiring future."[18]

My pastor of many years, Pastor Curtis A. Arnold, was a man of prayer and great vision. What the Holy Spirit spoke to him unveiled a clear vision within him. He then said, "I hear the sounds of the footsteps of the masses of people coming to the church." He heard them coming long before they arrived. And they arrived by the hundreds.

Pastor Arnold pastored a church of 350 people in Zanesville in the late 1950s which, at that time, would have been considered a mega church. He resigned from the church and moved back home to Frostproof, Florida. He wasn't there long before he realized he had missed God's will. He returned to Zanesville and started from scratch in pioneering a new church, Trinity Full Gospel. He had a vision of building a 1,000-seat sanctuary and in 1978 that vision was fulfilled. It is a testament to what faith in God and a clear vision can accomplish.

EXCEPTIONAL VISION

Prayer is the vehicle that takes us to a place of exceptional vision. My ophthalmologist asked me during my last visit if anybody had ever told me I had exceptional eyes. "No," I replied, "but what does that mean?" He said you have 20 x 15 vision. The best eyesight most people have is 20 x 20 vision. He went on to explain, in medical terms, what causes that. I still don't understand, but I'm very thankful for my great eyesight. Spiritually speaking, prayer opens our eyes into the Spirit's realm, and the Lord shows us what we need to see in order to accomplish His will. Like the eagle, we see farther than everybody else. We see what God is doing or is going to do. Prophet Kim Clement said at a revival service years ago, "I see you in the future and you look much better than you look right now." He quoted it, chanted it, and sang it that night, and the Holy Spirit moved in a mighty way. At times, I will look at somebody and begin to see them in the future: stronger, overcoming, and doing great things for God. Samuel had exceptional vision when he saw David. He saw a shepherd boy, yes, but he also saw him as the next King of Israel. It's when we are in prayer that our spiritual sight is heightened and enhanced to the level of the supernatural. Why settle for poor eyesight if you can have exceptional vision? Spend a little more time in prayer and you will see a lot better.

IF HE COULD SEE IT NOW

Many people have visited Disney World and stood in awe of the beauty of the creative design and imagination that went into its construction. After beholding Disney World, they make statements like, "If Walt Disney could see this beautiful place." Others reply, "He did." Disney had a vision and shared that vision the same year he died. "In 1966, Walt Disney announced his intention to build Epcot, an acronym for 'Experimental Prototype Community of Tomorrow.' It was to be no mere theme park, but as Disney put it, '... the creation of a living blueprint for the future, unlike anyplace else in the world,' an entire new city built from scratch."[19] It is everything Disney saw and so much more.

Even though we see in part, like Paul the Apostle said, we see so much more than others who do not look through the lenses of faith (See 2 Corinthians 3:18). The vision of faith enables us to see what others do not see, farther than others see, and clearer than others see.

What if you stayed at a hotel on the 18th floor for one week, and when you were checking out you overheard the person next to you request a room on the 38th floor? Before leaving, you take a tour of the 38th floor. You behold the beautiful view you lacked on the 18th floor. Leaving the hotel, you realize you saw much less the previous week than if you could have known better was possible.

God wants us to see clearly from His view. Through faith, we are able to see the vision as God sees it. In order to accomplish great things for God, we need the best vision of faith available. Similarly, don't be satisfied with low-level faith. If you have been living an 18th floor experience, check it out: there may be a 38th floor view of faith for your vision. Don't be satisfied to remain at one level of faith. We serve a God that has no limitations. Explore and experience the greatness of faith's possibilities.

VISION OPERATES THROUGH FAITH

CHAPTER SIX

Vision and faith go together like a horse and carriage. As the carriage goes nowhere without the horse, the vision goes nowhere without faith. The vision is received by faith and walked out by faith. It's been said that faith is hope for the future. Faith gives hope that we will see the fulfillment of the vision.

VISION STARTS SMALL

When the Lord gave me the vision for Cornerstone Church only a few people responded. These were influential people with a vision. It didn't take long before a great number of people followed. At that time, not one other person had started a church in Muskingum County. The step of faith to follow a vision spread and many others started churches in the years after. Whether it was the Lord, or people just thought that if Pastor Harrop could plant a church anybody could, I'm not sure. But one thing is for sure, God had given me a vision and it didn't matter how many people came to help, I was going to step out in faith.

You might say to yourself, well I don't have much faith. Jesus said if you have faith as small as a grain of mustard seed you can order the mountain to be cast into the sea and it will obey you (See Luke 17:6). The mustard seed is a tiny seed, but when planted it grows into a huge tree. Take that first step of faith and watch what God can do. All things are possible with God and those who believe. There is unlimited potential in faith put to action.

Sometimes we say we believe but then cancel out our prayers by speaking unbelief. Job 22:27- 29 says, "Thou shalt make thy prayer unto Him, and He shall hear thee, and thou shalt pay thy vows. Thou shalt also decree a thing, and it shall be established unto thee: and the light shall shine upon thy ways. When men are cast down, then thou shalt say: there is lifting up; and He shall save the humble person."

What promises the Lord gives us in these few verses! First, He says when we pray, He will hear us. No matter how we feel or the circumstances in our lives, He hears us. Second, God tells us to decree the things that we desire. The Hebrew word for decree is Gazar which means, "to divide, separate, destroy or decide." The definition reveals more of what happens in the spiritual realm. Third, God says what we say will be established and His light will shine upon our path. He will shine His light upon the path of vision and things will become clear to us. Finally, He says that we will lift people up by our prayers and the things we decree. People that are down need to be lifted up. True vision operating in faith moves mountains, sets captives free, and destroys the yoke of the enemy.

DARE TO BELIEVE

Will you dare to go boldly where no one has gone before? Vision requires us to be willing to go there. When we were little children playing with other kids, we would dare each other to do something. We would say, "I dare you to walk across that creek," or "I dare you to jump off the bridge into the river." Years after our son Jamie had graduated, he confessed that when he was in High School, he and his best friend Brian Smith jumped into the Muskingum River off the Gaysport bridge. Pat was shocked, and I just shook my head knowing teenage boys cannot turn down a dare. Now, if you were really brave you would double dare your buddy. Only the brave and fearless would accept that double dare! Spiritually speaking, are you willing to step out in faith and dare to obey God like Abraham? He was told by God to leave his home, family business, and follow God one step at a time to a place He would reveal to Abraham. No road map or GPS, just follow Me and I will bless you. God had a vision for Abraham, but it was given to him one phase at a time. You talk about a double dare! How was he going to explain this to his father and mother? He boldly walked away to follow God. "By faith Abraham, when he was called to go out unto a place which he should after receive for an inheritance, obeyed; and he went out, not knowing whither he went" (Hebrews 11:8).

HAPPY NEW YEAR

On Monday, January 1, 2024, Pastor Troy Ervin, a good friend, texted me the following encouraging word:

Isaiah 43:18-19, "Remember ye not the former things, neither consider the things of old. Behold, I will do a new thing; now it shall spring forth; shall ye not know it? I will even make a way in the wilderness, and rivers in the desert."

New things:

1. *The promise of it, "I will do a new thing."*
2. *The pouring forth of it, "It shall spring forth."*
3. *The perception of it, "Shall ye not know it?"*

It's going to be a year of favor where God does some new things in your life!

Happy New Year!

Before receiving Troy's text, I had been in prayer. I had just prayed for family, church family, and minister friends, including Troy. I texted a reply to Troy, and this is how the text went:

While thinking of you and whispering a prayer,

I want to wish you a Happy New Year, in all that you dare.

Dare to believe for God's new things.

Dare to believe for God's favor.

Dare to go where you have never been before.

Dare to trust God.

It will definitely be a Happy New Year when we dare to believe God to be all that He said He would be.

In Hebrews 11:6, "But without faith it is impossible to please Him: for he that cometh to God must believe that He is, and that He is a rewarder of them that diligently seek Him." You will never walk out vision until you trust God to do the things He said He will do and to be a rewarder to those who diligently seek Him.

WHAT IS VISION?

Galloway believes that "vision is faith bringing the future and present together" and that faith is seeing those things that are not before they become a reality. He provides as evidence Hebrews 11:1, "Now faith is the substance of things hoped for, the evidence of things not seen."[20]

The day your memories are greater than your dreams or visions is the day you quit advancing. Just like God told Moses to go forward He is telling us to move toward the vision. The Israelites kept wanting to look back at their memories. Moses the visionary wanted to launch forward by faith and see what God had in store for them. (See Exodus 14:15).

Apostle Les Bowling texts me a word of encouragement every Sunday morning. It is always uplifting, but he always caps it off with "Forward Steve!" There is nothing to go back to. Our past is behind us, we can't rewrite it. Our future is before us with possibilities as high as the heavens.

VISION WITH RISK

The turtle is one of God's unique creatures. John Maxwell tells the story of a turtle that challenges me to go all in: "He only moves ahead when he has his neck stuck out. I do not know why, but the only times a church shows much progress is when it sticks its neck out a little further."[21] Advancing God's Kingdom comes with courageous steps that few are willing to take.

My good friend Rick Van Wagner pastors a great church in Clermont, Florida. He pioneered the church in 1998. He told me that at first he and his staff couldn't get people to come to church, but he had a vision of a great church in Clermont. They kept praying and remained faithful to the call and all at once they couldn't hold all the people coming to church. People were getting saved and being discipled in Christ. Rick has always been a man who didn't shy away from taking a risk. He started a daycare and it prospered. While doing one building project after another he trusted God for the finances. Next came a Christian School that now has 600 students in grades kindergarten through twelfth. A few years ago, the Lord gave Rick a vision for a Sky Zone connected to their sanctuary. I'm sure it came with some resistance, but he built it following the vision. In no time the Sky Zone was packed constantly. By faith, they added to the present structure. The blessings are that the kids are able to use it after the church services and the structure draws thousands of people onto their property where they can be influenced with the gospel. True vision always requires risk.

When we built our first sanctuary, the bank required 30

families to sign as co-signers. As my wife and I signed, we both felt the weight that came along with putting our family at risk - but thirty families? Even though it was a risk, like the turtle, we stuck our necks out to see the Kingdom advanced. We paid the mortgage off in five years. Many of those co-signers believed in us enough and trusted God that on the second sanctuary, many were willing to sign again. God rewards risk-takers.

The year was 1966 when my dad said to me, "Steve, you have graduated from Jr. High so I'm going to take you to Montgomery Ward in Zanesville. You can pick out any motorcycle you want for your graduation gift." I was on cloud nine to say the least. While I loved Montgomery Ward because of the bike, I found that my appreciation for its merchandise declined when a larger store made its appearance. Even though Montgomery Ward was a nice store, the Sears and Roebuck Store was much bigger because Sears risked much to gain much. Maxwell points out how this applies to working God's Kingdom: "If you ever stop going for it, then you stop being effective for God. Success is a process."[22]

Any leader who is willing to lay it all on the line and risk all he has for the gospel will be rewarded. That investment is faith in action. Every step we take is a step of faith. There is risk on every corner so every decision must be bathed in prayer. Many moves in the natural seem ridiculous, but that's where faith comes in. Jesus never let the natural laws stop Him from walking on water.

At every juncture of advancement, there is risk. Pastors are not just building for the present but for the future. In 1998 we were not building for the 20th century because we had a vision for future growth. Now we realize it was for a time as this. I love the quote: "Faith seems to come more easily when I assume in advance that God wants to reveal His plans for our lives."[23]

With new ideas comes vulnerability to critics who say, "We've never done this before." However, risks have great rewards when led by the Holy Spirit. Risks must be taken; confrontations must be made. In A Word from the Wise, I.D. Thomas emphasizes why this must be so with his story of a risk-averse Georgia farmer living in a dilapidated shack. "A stranger asked, 'How's your cotton doing?' 'Aint got none,' said the farmer. Fraid of boll weevils.' "How's your corn?' 'Didn't plant none. Fraid there wasn't gonna be no rain.' 'Really, what did you plant?' 'Nothin' was the reply, I just played it safe.' "[24]

The church that is never willing to take a risk will reap no return. In Proverbs 6:6-15, the sluggard is warned of no rewards. Jesus' parable of the talents tells of the three different investors. The first two took a risk and doubled their master's money. The third, out of fear, buried his master's money. Soon the day of accountability came. God rewards those who take the risk of faith. It is not blind foolish faith; it is faith based on His Word and vision (See Matthew 25:14-30).

Years ago, when we were making plans to build our first sanctuary, many opinions were voiced concerning where we would get the money. Everybody agreed we needed a building of our own. Some doubted we could borrow the money, while others were opposed to dealing with banks. To one man banks were evil and we should have nothing to do with banks. However, he offered no solution as to where we would get the finances to build. To him, it was too much of a risk to borrow the amount of money needed. Every step I had taken in the starting and building of a church had been a risk. I've always considered the risk Jesus took on me and nothing is too great a risk when serving Him.

People who refuse to take risks seldom ever accomplish anything purposeful in life. They come to the end of their lives and look back thinking, what if I had given it my all and took a risk with what God gave me. Not me! My life is in Jesus' hands. I'm determined to make this life count for Him without reservations. Psychologist John Atkinson showed that "those motivated to achieve generally take regular, consistent, and intermediate risks. Those motivated to avoid failure... avoid risk altogether, or they make extremely risky moves."[25]

Let's revisit the ministry of Jesus. His entire life was a risk. From His birth and Herod's attempt to kill Him, to the religious leaders trying to throw Him off a cliff ... His life was threatened. Jesus was willing to take the risk of dying. But knowing the reward of conquering death instructed Him to lay His life down. The risk paid off, thank God... He's alive.

Paul was not shy about taking risks either. In Acts 20:24, we see his courage: "But none of these things move me, neither count I my life dear unto myself, so that I may finish my course with joy, and the ministry, which I have received of the Lord Jesus, to testify the gospel of the grace of God."

Jesus and Paul motivate me to lay my life on the line.

RISKS WITH NO REWARD

There is so much truth in Fred Smith's short story:

"Once in New York City, I looked out my hotel window and saw several teenagers walking an 18-inch ledge, thirty stories up, with no hand railing to grab... (This) principle of calculating the risk is seen in the verse, 'What good will it be for a man if he gains the whole world, yet forfeits his soul?' The benefits of temporary gain are offset by permanent loss."[26]

Any major move or decision made in the church should be confirmed by wise counsel, bathed in prayer, and the peace of God echoing a resounding amen. We have all scratched our heads at decisions some people make and wonder what they were thinking. Somebody new to our church said to me recently, "I have noticed that nothing is done at Cornerstone in a hurry. Everything is methodically, slowly, and well thought out." Usually, the school of hard knocks works that discipline out in a person's life. We give great advice to children to stop, look and listen. We should take our own advice. Stop, don't get in a hurry. Look around and see what others have done. Listen to wise counsel and God's voice. The number one filter to run decisions through is the Word of God. If it doesn't line up with the Word, don't risk it.

For many years older mainline denominations bucked the idea of contemporary Christian music. The older people held to their hymns and southern gospel music. The result has been catastrophic for many churches. They couldn't see the risk was worth the potential reward. Younger people tend to lean toward contemporary Christian music. Many have pulled away from the traditional style of worship and others have sought out churches that have worship singing more to their liking. The risk of refusal to adapt to the times can be very costly. Do your homework and weigh out the risk versus the reward. I encourage you to be willing to take a risk when God gives you the green light. Don't stand still when God says to walk on the water.

WHAT IF?

- What if Abraham had not been willing to take the risk?
- There would be no Israel.
- What if David had not been willing to refuse to compromise?
- There would be no latter-day prophecies.
- What if Noah had not been willing to take a risk?
- There would be no world today.
- What if Jesus had not been willing to take a risk?
- There would be no salvation.
- What if Tom Thompson had not been willing to take a risk?
- There would be no Refuge Ministries.

- What if the Cornerstone family had not been willing to take a risk?
- Would there be a Cornerstone Church today?

VISIONARY LEADERS

CHAPTER SEVEN

It is true that everything rises and falls on leadership. Without a head the body goes nowhere. With strong leadership vision will rise to the height of its purpose, but without it vision will fade away into the sunset of despair. Leadership is the ability to lead the ship in the right direction with the help of its crew.

As a young Christian, I had a great desire to learn and grow as a leader. My pastor was a great preacher and role model. He was a great leader in many ways. His greatest attribute was his work ethic. He could outwork a man half his age. In those days there was little emphasis on leadership. In so many ways it seemed to come naturally to him. It wasn't until we started Cornerstone Church that I realized that I lacked good leadership skills. After several years, it was obvious our church lacked strong leadership, too. We first began to pray about leaders, and then the Lord gave us a plan to develop and delegate leaders. The vision was coming together so fast, but I was still as green as grass concerning leadership development.

I learned the hard way not to overwork good people in the church. We had a young couple who loved children and offered to care for the children. We called it junior church. They did a great job working with the kids on Sunday mornings, Sunday nights, and Wednesday nights for about a year. They became burned out, and we lost them. It was a valuable lesson learned. Don't allow anybody to work a ministry that keeps them out of church all the time. When a person gives out, they must be fed themselves. At Cornerstone Church, we have two Sunday morning services. Pastor Sheryl Alexander coordinates our nursery and Jr. Church. She is worth her weight in gold! We are blessed with two junior church teams that enable each team to experience a worship service and work the other. We try to keep the reins on even the hardest workers for their safety and spiritual well-being.

BEGIN WITH THE BASICS

As a leader, my greatest goal is always to grow and develop; not just in my gift of teaching and preaching, but in character and holiness as well. There are many resources available to aid our growth but spending time with God and in His Word are the greatest. When we cease to grow, we stop improving our staff. Growth is time well invested. Over the years of pastoring, I was hit and miss when it came to spending quality time with my staff. Being too involved in the nuts and bolts of the ministry and most of the pastoral care robbed the staff of my time. My old-school training said the pastor does all the visiting, praying, and counseling. That left little time and energy for my staff.

Eventually, I sensed a distancing of my staff. One of them got really honest with me one day. He said, "Pastor, I love you, but I'm starting to feel more like a hired hand than a spiritual son." I apologized to him and promised to start spending more time with the staff. That was many years ago and I have learned to give my best time to them. We have grown to be like family at church, and we go places together several times a year. We meet every week at 10 am on Tuesday mornings. We're never done by noon. We discuss everything going on in the church from pastoral care, new members, purchases, weekend recap, current events, and strategy for future events. I value our time spent and the great wisdom that comes out of those meetings. Those are the most important meetings of the week. The staff at Cornerstone has never been closer or stronger. We are growing together. The men of the staff take a week off to go to Florida together every winter. It is time well spent resting from ministry obligations, connecting with one another, some spiritual refreshing time and just having fun together - oh, and eating often. When we are eating, our conversation is always centered around where we will be served our next meal. It is always my goal to encourage and give some guidance to the staff. They get lots of love and small doses of correction only when it is necessary. To me, correction is more encouragement to look at something in a different way. I never tell a staff member they are a disappointment to me. I always encourage them to let it be a good learning experience so they will be a better person or leader.

VISIONARIES ARE LED BY REVELATION

"Henceforth I call you not servants; for the servant knoweth not what his lord doeth: but I have called you friends; for all things that I have heard of my Father I have made known unto you" (John 15:15). In Jesus' mind and heart, He elevated His disciples from servants to friends. Would they still serve Him? Yes, out of relationship and friendship they would serve Him. Jesus told them everything the Father had told Him. This enabled them to know what to do and where to serve the Father. We should never attempt to lead without listening to the Holy Spirit who relays the heart of Jesus and the Father. Visionary leaders are led by revelation from the Father. How comforting to know that we are not groping in the dark trying to serve God alone. Paul said, "We are laborers together with God" (1 Corinthians 3:9a). As we learn to trust our Father we walk in confidence and boldness.

All pastors need to seek God for His direction or the church is like a ship without a rudder. It wanders aimlessly, failing to reach its destination, spinning around in circles. You cannot lead if you don't know where you are going. Syncretistic beliefs are blended beliefs that confuse the Bible with other belief systems. For example, "On May 16, 2022, George Barna presented the Arizona Christian University survey of 1000 Christian pastors. This revealed that about 1/3 had a biblical world vision but nearly 2/3 had a Syncretistic 'hybrid' world vision. Among Executive Pastors, only 4% 'have consistently biblical beliefs.' Among Senior Pastors, 41% possessed a biblical world vision."[27] Pastors: it is time for biblical visionary leadership.

Such secular-Christian hybrid pastors might do well to consider the words of the economist Milton Friedman, "One of the great mistakes is to judge policies and programs by their intentions rather than their results." The Bible got us unity and the salvation of Christ. Secularism brings only inconsistency, conflict, and tribalism.

FOLLOWING THE VISIONARY LEADER

I am honored to be a leader that people choose to follow. I realize many people pass by many churches to drive to ours. There are many great leaders in our area they could follow but they choose to follow Cornerstone. Like Paul said, "Follow me as I follow Christ" (See 1 Corinthians 11:1 English Standard Version ESV). People will follow the man or woman who genuinely follows Christ and refuses to compromise the Word of God. The Holy Spirit leads people to follow us and that is humbling. That responsibility should be received with fear and trembling. When I started full-time ministry in April of 1981, I realized I would either encourage or discourage people to be a follower of Christ. That reality keeps me on my toes, knowing accountability is coming. Leadership success is marked by two external characteristics: integrity and followers.

VISIONARY LEADERS INFLUENCE

Someone has said that leadership is influence. The greatest kind of leadership is being able to influence those who in turn influence everyone else. Gaining and maintaining influence has to do with recognizing and utilizing your basic leadership inclinations and strengths. There are two distinct kinds of leaders. First, there is the cohesive leader who creates togetherness and warm, fuzzy relationships. These people are highly relational. Then there is the task leader. He or she has visions, sets goals, and goes all out to accomplish the dream. The task leader makes a congregation believe that the task will be accomplished somehow. If you are a task leader, you need to try to be more cohesive. If you are a cohesive leader, you need to become more task- focused. Both cohesive and task leaders are needed in the church. Most pastors generally appreciate only one or the other. We need to value both.

HOW DO PEOPLE GET THEIR INFLUENCE?

Influencers project these traits:

- Clear vision - Vision that is easily understood and aggressively followed.
- Credibility - Being a person of your word. A person is indeed only as good as their word.
- Confidence - Allows people with great faith to lead the way.
- Character - Actions and attitude speak as loudly, if not more loudly, than words; a leader has to model ministry to teach ministry.
- Commitment - Speaks louder than words. It is easier caught than taught.

- Courage – People will not follow a person if their leader is not committed to the vision one hundred percent.
- Gifting – In order to be a good influencer, one must be gifted and faithful.
- Sacrificing – Influencers are willing to sacrifice all for the vision.

In World War II Lieutenant Dick Williams led his troops over the knoll of a hill in Karentown, France into the line of fire of two machine guns. Into the ditch his troops went. Williams went from ditch-to-ditch yelling, "Advance or die." They advanced and won. Later he was asked why he risked his life and he replied, "I believe leaders lead." True leaders are willing to lead at all costs. They see what it will take to motivate the people and are willing to sacrifice to get the job done.

LEVELS OF LEADERSHIP

Good wisdom says don't buy a car without reverse - you might need to back up. Leaders sometimes need to back up. When a leader makes a mistake, he or she should be quick to take ownership of their mistake. I have discovered that people will highly respect you when you take ownership of your mistakes. It is hard to follow a leader who has too much pride to admit errors. A study was done of the most successful businesses in the U.S.A. Three values were found in all of them:

- A core of values established to offer the best service.
- A relentless drive for progress to do more.
- Strength beyond the strength of one individual as a team.

Visionary leaders set the bar high for excellence in ministry. Never be satisfied with average. Sometimes settling for good is the enemy of the best. Paul said, "Whatever you do, do it heartily as unto the Lord" (See Colossians 3:23). I truly believe every believer is called to full-time ministry. Everybody has a pulpit and a platform. Yours might be at a steel mill, a salon, a farm, or a church. Use your influence for the glory of God to influence people into the kingdom and into being an influencer.

MOSES: THE VISIONARY LEADER

In Exodus 18:13-27 we see the wisdom of Moses in listening to his father-in-law. Moses was trying to do it all by counseling everybody who needed advice. The problem was there were three million Israelites. Moses was wearing himself and the people out as they stood in long lines waiting their turn to speak to him. Jethro encouraged Moses to choose teachable men with good character and train them well: men who fear God, love truth, and hate covetousness. Moses did as Jethro said and trained the men. I commend Moses for taking wise counsel from his father-in-law. Jethro was a spiritual father to Moses; one that loved him and wanted to see him succeed.

Surround yourself with good wise people that aren't afraid to help you when you need some guidance.

Galloway describes three problems in today's Church: burnout, dissatisfaction, and unhealthy self-reliance.[28] My personal approach to these follows:

- Burnout: I see this as one of the biggest problems in the church. Beware of overload. A truck may be built to haul five tons, but if you continue to haul 10 tons on it, eventually it will break down. People are like that dump truck. We can only carry so much, or we too will break down. Some people are broken beyond repair. Don't let your church workers hurt themselves. Spread out the load. Work smarter, not harder. Learn to pace yourself, relax, and spend valuable time with family.

- Dissatisfaction: Most unhappy church people are dissatisfied because they have no "skin in the game." We solve this with multiple activities that are overseen but not run by the Pastor. We have another important tool: people consistently witness in the various groups so that they feel welcomed by the church members the moment they first walk in the door. This best occurs when people are trained on how to welcome and greet people.

- Unhealthy Self-Reliance: So many of us think if it's going to get done right, I have to do it. Reality says one person can't do it all. It's always a good idea to learn to delegate. Why? Because delegating multiplies yourself. Doing this saves your life and gives meaning to others.

ONE VISIONARY LEADER

My experience of vision for the church has been that God gives vision to only one person. I knew little about vision for the corporate body when the Lord showed me the vision of Cornerstone. He didn't give it to a committee or board, he gave it to one man. I can very well see why the Lord gives vision to one. To give it to multiple people, everybody would interpret it differently. It would leave vision open to debate.

An important Biblical example of this unipolar leadership was Moses. God had a mammoth task for Moses and got his attention through a supernatural sign. In Exodus 3:1-10, the Lord met with Moses at the burning bush that was not consumed. Moses' response was to draw near and see what this burning bush meant. The Lord told him to take his shoes off for the place was holy ground. This is a sign of reverence, humility, and respect which God requires for His servants to draw near. Moses' response was to hide his face in utter humility. The Lord told Moses the reason for this encounter: I have seen the affliction of my people and I am come to deliver them from Egyptian bondage. You are the man I am going to use. The Lord didn't appear to a committee; he made Himself and the vision known to one faithful man.

We see this principle repeatedly in scripture. God spoke to Noah, not a committee, to build the Ark. He spoke to David, not a building committee, about the plans for building the Temple. He spoke to Paul, not a committee, to go to Philippi to start a church.

Joel C. Hunter said, "In twenty years of ministry, I have never seen a committee receive vision. Committees have offered wonderful methods to accomplish a vision or reach a goal. They have confirmed and refined an individual's insights. But I have never seen vision originate in group process – not in the Bible, not in the church."[29]

Paul knew he was called to missions work for the Gentiles. "And I said, Who art thou, Lord? And he said, I am Jesus whom thou persecutest. But rise, and stand upon thy feet; for I have appeared unto thee for this purpose, to make thee a minister and a witness both of these things which thou hast seen, and of those things in which I will appear unto thee; delivering thee from the people, and from the Gentiles, unto whom now I send thee" (Acts 26:15-17).

However, Paul waited for the confirmation of the Apostolic Leaders at Antioch:

> "Now there were in the church that was at Antioch certain prophets and teachers; as Barnabas, and Simeon that was called Niger, and Lucius of Cyrene, and Manaen, which had been brought up with Herod the tetrarch, and Saul. As they ministered to the Lord, and fasted, the Holy Ghost said, Separate me Barnabas and Saul for the work whereunto I have called them. And when they had fasted and prayed, and laid their hands on them, they sent them away. So they, being sent forth by the Holy Ghost, departed unto Seleucia; and from thence they sailed to Cyprus" (Acts 13:1-4).

God gave vision to Paul, one man, concerning his mission's call. When the time was right, it was confirmed by the Holy Ghost through Apostolic Leaders. I have seen many ministers leave one church to go to another without being sent by good pastoral leadership. The outcome isn't always favorable. There is safety in the prayerful counsel of leaders led by the Holy Ghost. Follow the visionary leader that has received vision from God and has the witness of the Spirit and credentials to prove it.

HINDRANCES TO VISION

CHAPTER EIGHT

Looking back on my life as a minister and visionary, I realize some decisions I made greatly hindered and others greatly enhanced God's vision. We would all like to rethink and redo some things. Thank God we have made more good decisions than bad. In my early days of ministry, my greatest weakness was during times of little prayer, sometimes bordering on prayerlessness. It is hard to lead God's ship when we are not praying about every move. We see best through the eyes of prayer.

The Lord shows us warning signs and gives us unique insight into strategic moves in ministry when we pray. Jesus modeled a life of prayer. He would rise early before dawn to spend time with the Father praying, listening, and watching His every move. Before Jesus chose His disciples He prayed all night. He told His disciples to go before Him over the sea so He could slip away and pray to the Father. He prayed in the Garden of Gethsemane asking for another way other than drinking the cup, but then surrendered to the Father's will. Paul instructed us to "Pray without ceasing" (I Thessalonians 5:17). Israel's next move after defeating Jericho was to go to the city of Ai and conquer it. Their big mistake was they failed to pray first. They were overconfident in thinking Ai was a small city so they didn't need to send up all of their troops. How soon we forget Who fights our battles. Israel's troops didn't win the victory at Jericho, it was God. When we put our confidence in our flesh or our own abilities, we set ourselves up for failure. Pray like it all depends on God - because it does.

HINDRANCES WITHIN US

Sometimes we can't get out of our own way. When the hindrance is me, the vision suffers. There are many battles we fight with weaknesses of the flesh. As leaders, we must "be strong in the Lord and in the power of His might" (Ephesians 6:10). Our faith and our moral character must also be strong: "That He would grant you, according to the riches of His glory, to be strengthened with might by His Spirit in the inner man" (Ephesians 3:16).

One of the greatest hindrances we fight is fear. No wonder some 365 times in the Bible God tells us to fear not. Fear is very tormenting to the heart and mind of the believer. When left unchecked it can erode your faith. Fear of failure is also counterproductive. Instead of motivating a person to work harder, it actually cripples any person who relies on their intellect. That's because the natural man cannot know the things of the Spirit.

My son Jamie testified that the greatest reason he didn't get saved until 2007 was the fear of failure. When Evangelist Chris Owensby preached about the fear of failure, Jamie knew the Lord had him in his sights. Many pastors allow fear to control them. They refuse to take a risk for fear of being wrong. I had many thoughts of inadequacies that plagued me as a child. At my conversion, most of that left me because of knowing and experiencing His awesome power. Colossians 2:10 says, "And ye are complete in Him." Christ fills up the empty chasms of inadequacy in our lives. There are also feelings of inadequacies caused by the many heartbreaking experiences we see in ministry. I have learned to commit them to the Lord knowing I can't heal them, but I am confident He can.

Conversely, it's been said, "Fear not failure, beware of success." Success feeds the flesh of pride. Solomon once said, "Pride goes before destruction." Check your heart for any signs of pride, because it is a huge hindrance to vision. Settle it in your heart that any success achieved in this ministry comes from the Lord.

Another hindrance to vision is celebrating our past victories too long. When God gives you a victory, don't "spike the ball" and do a celebration dance. Be humble and recognize the victory came from God. There are great needs remaining that require future successes.

And then there is the hindrance of unforgiveness in many visionaries. Jonah is a great example of a man who would not forgive the Ninevites. Their ancestors had persecuted the Israelites and Jonah hated them (See Jonah 1-4). Unforgiveness as well as a spirit of offense will enslave a person. Jonah ran from the presence of the Lord when the Lord told him to go to Nineveh and preach repentance to the city. As a result of unforgiveness, he finds himself in the belly of a whale for three days: a very uncomfortable, scary place to be. There he prayed and the Lord had the whale spit him out. Unforgiveness will affect you and others around you until you forgive from your heart. The Lord will not forgive us until we are willing to forgive others (See Matthew 18:35).

Another great hindrance to vision is doubt and unbelief. If God gives the promise and He has fulfilled His promises in the past, why should we doubt Him? Look at all the times He has come through for us. Think about the promise of countless descendants the Lord gave to Abraham (Genesis 17:2). Abraham's heart was filled with excitement and gratitude. Even though Sarah doubted and she laughed, she quickly returned to faith. Never allow doubt to blind you to God's amazing vision for your life or ministry. It is always difficult when some people in the church have great faith but others struggle with trusting God. When the twelve spies went into Canaan to spy out the land, they came back with different opinions. All saw the same thing, but some believed they could take the land and others didn't: "And Caleb stilled the people before Moses, and said, Let us go up at once, and possess it; for we are well able to overcome it. But the men that went up with him said, We be not able to go up against the people; for they are stronger than we" (Numbers 13:30-31). We only see the giants when God is left out. There are many challenges to our vision, but faith in God will always see the possibilities over the problems.

Another hindrance to vision is attitude. The person who always sees the glass half empty seldom sees anything good. They are negative and a drain on a business or a church. Attitude will make or break you and determine effectiveness in everything you do. Have you ever asked yourself why, in church, we so often overlook attitudes? Attitudes determine altitudes.

You can be equal in talent but poor in attitude and you won't get the job done. The other person with a good attitude will. Attitude is a difference maker.

A WRONG MOTIVE HINDERS THE VISION

Tommy Barnett says, "The only thing that can stop a church from growing is a wrong motive."[30] A wrong motive seeks glory. God will not bless the heart contaminated with a wrong motive. A church can have the best music, the best talent, and the best preaching, but without a pure heart and motive, the blessing of the Lord will always be missing. Jesus dealt with James and John about motive. He scolded them saying, "You don't know what manner of spirit ye are of" (Luke 9:55). A wrong motive was seen in the Pharisees and religious leaders of Jesus' days. God loves a pure heart with the right motives.

PROCRASTINATION STOPS VISION

When people procrastinate, the job never gets done. "One of these days" never comes. How often do you hear of someone who died and didn't have a will prepared? They mentioned for years they were going to get a will made, but it just never got done. Assets are frozen and the state laws determine where their property goes.

Similarly, souls are lost for eternity because somebody procrastinated and put off telling their neighbor about Jesus. The devil never says people don't need to hear about Jesus. He does say another day, not now. Procrastination will not only hinder a vision; it will stop it because "one of these days" never arrives. My philosophy is why put something off until tomorrow if I can do it today. Be a step ahead of the game and be a winner. A true passion to fulfill the vision is necessary and breaks "first step" procrastination. Each step builds momentum until you cross the finish line.

HINDRANCES AROUND US

In any ministry, there will always be people around us that do their best to hinder us or stop us. Prior to starting the church in 1986, a minister called to congratulate me. He said, "It's about time you are stepping out and doing something for the Lord." Shortly after we launched Cornerstone Church, he called again. This time was different. He had heard how many people were attending the services. He credited my charismatic personality as the reason people were coming and made some false accusations. I told him I was sorry he felt that way and wished him a nice day. I couldn't believe the accusations launched against me. One accusation was that I was proselyting members of other churches. The Lord knew my heart and character. I had been saved for eleven years and had never operated by using such practices. I had seen others do it and recognized that it was wrong. I still hold to that standard, respect other pastors, and fear the Lord enough to keep me from such tactics.

We may differ, but I choose to love and forgive. The Lord let me know that He would fight my battles. He has been faithful. My pastor used to say, "I don't mind fighting the devil but I'm not going to fight other believers."

THERE WILL ALWAYS BE PERSECUTION

We are living in a day of great persecution. The devil knows his time is short and he is unleashing all of hell against the church of Jesus Christ. Persecution has always followed true gospel preaching. Persecution has never stopped the church but rather motivated it to keep on preaching the gospel. In the Book of Acts, the church thanked God they were worthy to suffer shame for His Name (Acts 5:41). The weak will always run from persecution while the strong will run to it. Jesus suffered rejection and persecution even from His own family. He warned us that if they hated Me, they would hate you. Yet, "Rejoice and be exceedingly glad, for great is your reward in heaven" (Matt 5:12a). I greatly admire those who are taking the gospel into foreign countries where believers are martyred for their faith. They are the true heroes of the faith.

HINDRANCES OF IN-HOUSE DIVISIONS

It is no surprise Jesus spoke so openly about divisions. The Pharisees accused Jesus of having a devil because He cast devils out of people. Matthew 12:25-28 provides His response:

"And Jesus knew their thoughts, and said unto them, Every kingdom divided against itself is brought to desolation; and every city or house divided against itself shall not stand: and if Satan cast out Satan, he is divided against himself; how shall then his kingdom stand? And if I by Beelzebub cast out devils, by whom do your children cast them out? But if I cast out devils by the Spirit of God, then the kingdom of God is come unto you."

Division means two visions. It means to split, partition, and disunify. A house, business, or church cannot stand if there is division. Two visions will eventually create a split or division. The first place we see the destructive force of division is in heaven. Lucifer, the most beautiful angel God had created, became full of pride. He schemed to overtake God's throne. When the Lord detected his heart was corrupt, He instantly kicked him out of heaven (See Isaiah 14:12, and Luke 10:18). Division cannot be tolerated in any place, especially in God's church. It only thinks of itself with its own agenda not caring about God's vision. Division can set a church back for many years and sometimes it never fully recovers. We all have to ask ourselves the question, "Am I part of the problem or part of the solution?" God's vision is more important than any differences we may have. If we seek God with our whole heart, He will bring us to the unity of the Spirit. Love will keep us together.

Cornerstone has survived divisions in the past. I will not go into the gory details; that would not be fruitful or glorify God. I will share how we made it though. It is always a very painful process. It is similar to a divorce I am told. With God's help and grace, Pat and I have never experienced that. Anytime any of us lose something we value, we grieve.

Whether it's the death of a loved one, the loss of a job, or the loss of people leaving the church, we grieve. During some of these events exaggerations occur, hurtful things are said, or occasionally painful lies are told. The only way to stop the bleeding and for healing to begin is to forgive. That is a choice. Every time we feel pain and anger, we must pull the trigger of forgiveness. That may work a blister on your trigger finger, but it releases the offender into the Lord's hands and off of your chopping block of revenge. It is then that the peace of God floods our hearts and minds. If you refuse to pick the scab and allow God to heal you, you will eventually be able to see God's redemptive plan. Choose to be better, not bitter. What a joy to be able to report we have weathered the storms of divisions with no animosity and genuine love in our hearts for everyone. You see, the bottom line is that we are Christians and God loves His children. Even when we are at odds with each other, He loves us and wants us to glorify Him and work differences out. I believe Christians should be the first to forgive and make peace.

UNRESOLVED CONFLICT

Unresolved conflict can and will have a negative outcome on any church. It is never easy or comfortable to confront issues, but left unresolved they will slowly hemorrhage the life of the church for years to come. Jesus gave us the formula to solve conflicts in the church, the home, or on the job. In Matthew 18:15-18, Jesus tells us:

> "Moreover if thy brother shall trespass against thee, go and tell him his fault between thee and him alone: if he shall hear thee, thou hast gained thy brother. But if he will not hear thee, then take with thee one or two more, that in the mouth of two or three witnesses every word may be established. And if he shall neglect to hear them, tell it unto the church: but if he neglect to hear the church, let him be unto thee as an heathen man and a publican. Verily I say unto you, Whatsoever ye shall bind on earth shall be bound in heaven: and whatsoever ye shall loose on earth shall be loosed in heaven."

Unresolved conflict will only fester and get worse if left unchecked. It is only through tough love confronting problems head-on that things can be resolved. This will glorify the Lord, and peace will be restored if handled in the correct way. Always remember there are two sides to every problem. Hear them both out before coming to conclusions and acting.

UNREWARDED EFFORT

Another issue that can hinder the vision is unrewarded effort. A pat on the back and thank you always fits. Recently, all of our staff members wrote an appreciation card to every person involved in any ministry at the church. I received thanks from many and even some that I didn't think it would mean much. Everybody wants to be loved and appreciated. It encourages people to work harder, be faithful, and pass the blessing on. A man at our church who was the CEO of a large corporation once told me, "Your employees won't remember how much time you spend with them, but they will never forget you took time to stop and give them a hand." He said that while making his rounds throughout the coal mine he stopped and helped each man for a few minutes, and asked how they and their families were doing. This built a great love, appreciation, and bond between them.

Sometimes, in the church, people volunteer faithfully for years without a "thank you" or "You are doing a great job." "I appreciate you," are words that never grow old. When someone does you a favor, always acknowledge that person. A verbal "thank you", a thank you card, or even a gift card to reward a job well done encourages a person to continue serving in their ministry. Such tokens of appreciation also teach others how to show appreciation as well.

SPIRITUAL WARFARE

Those who are well versed in the scriptures realize the part that spiritual warfare plays in hindering vision. Every time we seek to advance in our spiritual walk with Christ or move forward with God's plan the enemy opposes us. The enemy's strategies have not changed from the Garden of Eden to the

Garden of Gethsemane. He still attempts to trample our garden down. Let's look at Paul's writings: 1 Thessalonians 2:18, "Wherefore we would have come to you, even I Paul, once and again; but Satan hindered us." Again in Ephesians 6:12 we see, "For we wrestle not against flesh and blood, but against principalities, against powers, against the rulers of the darkness of this world, against spiritual wickedness in high places." Notice what James says about little spats in the church body:

> "But if ye have bitter envying and strife in your hearts, glory not, and lie not against the truth. This wisdom descendeth not from above, but is earthly, sensual, devilish. For where envying and strife is, there is confusion and every evil work. But the wisdom that is from above is first pure, then peaceable, gentle, and easy to be intreated, full of mercy and good fruits, without partiality, and without hypocrisy" (James 3:14-17).

It was revealed to Daniel by the Lord Himself that Satan, the prince of the Kingdom of Persia, had hindered him from receiving answers to his prayers. For 21 days Daniel fasted and then the Lord appeared to him. Daniel's response was to fall on his face, seeing his own shortcomings. Then the Lord touched him and helped him up on his knees and told him he was greatly beloved by the Lord. At that time truth was revealed to him about spiritual warfare. (See Daniel 10). It is important to keep our guard up because our "adversary the devil, as a roaring lion, walketh about, seeking whom he may devour" (1 Peter 5:8). One should "not give the devil a foothold" (Ephesians 4:27 NIV). United we stand, divided we fall. Don't give the devil an inch.

SPIRITUAL GREATNESS

I have heard the statement "That is good enough" many times. When it comes to God's work, good is not good enough. When we strive for perfection, we will never attain it, but we will hit right below it on excellence. You have heard it said that the enemy of greatness is good. Why be satisfied with good when you can live in greatness with God? I have never been content with average when better and best are possibilities. An "average" effort cannot be lived with. I vow to learn from my lack of effort and, with God's help and grace, do better the next time. God's people are so filled with gratitude that they want to do something great for God. They need shown that within them is the Spirit of greatness. Anybody can be great by being a servant. Paul said, "By love serve one another" (Galatians 5:13b). When we see ourselves as servants, barriers and hindrances are removed which allows us to work towards greatness for God.

CASTING THE VISION

CHAPTER NINE

Casting vision is like selling a car. You have to believe you have the car the buyer needs. The vision of the gospel is the best, most dependable ride in life that will take you into the next life. I'm not a salesman, but I believe in the vision of Jesus the Christ and I have spread the good news for forty-nine years. I'm sold on the fact that God loves every human being enough that he sacrificed His one and only Son so that no one would have to perish, but that all could be saved (See John 3:16-17). If you believe it, spread it!

VISION CASTING TAKES PASSION

It has been said that nothing is ever accomplished without enthusiasm. If you're not excited about the vision, nobody else will be either. Enthusiasm is the fuel that powers the engine of the vision. Habakkuk 2:2 reinforces this: "And the Lord answered me, and said, Write the vision, and make it plain upon tables, that he may run that readeth it." It was God who gave the vision to Habakkuk. If God gives it, it will be exciting and life changing. We need to write down the vision and keep it simple. The simplicity of the gospel makes it easy to understand

and if we understand it, we can run with it. I am honored to work with a staff and a church that are passionate about Christ. Everything revolves around Him. He is the center of everything. Every gift, every ministry, every song, every sermon, and every testimony flows out of and for Him. As Colossians 2:10 puts it, "And ye are complete in Him, (Christ) which is the head of all principality and power." Our passion is in Christ, not religion or tradition of man.

Everything we set out to support is designed to enthusiastically promote the true vision. In Exodus 14:13-16, Moses was motivated by God's vision of parting the Red Sea and Israel crossing on dry land. King Saul was passionate about the vision of amassing an Army to fight the Ammonites. He told the men to come and fight or he would slay their oxen – just as he slew a yoke of oxen before them. His passionate leadership inspired the men to form an army of 330,000 men to defeat the enemy (I Samuel 11:6-8). The vision would have gone nowhere if King Saul had not been passionate. A vision for the lost will drive you to your knees in prayer. It will take you out of your comfort zone to invite them to church or to help them to know Christ. It will give you the courage to rise up and be bold like the passionate One. Casting vision begins with the heart. It will compel you to do the uncommon or even the extraordinary.

Years ago in Zanesville, Ohio, a local pastor who had served in a church for years testified that he came under conviction and got saved. He was so passionate about his salvation that he went door-to-door witnessing Christ's saving power. I know that because he led a friend of mine to Christ. Oh, that the church of Jesus Christ worldwide had that love and zeal for

Christ that would take us past our fears to witness for Him! The world needs us to be His ambassador. I have watched many people get on fire for God and His vision down through the years. Two of those men are friends who greatly inspire me: Mike McGuire, pastor of Rushing Wind Biker Church, and Gary Phipps.

Mike has a love and zeal for lost bikers like none I have ever seen. He knows all the local bikers' clubs and their leaders. He is greatly loved and appreciated by them. When they have prayer requests or one of them dies, it is Mike that they call. Poker runs are seldom started without Mike asking God's blessing on their bikes. He has influenced many with the gospel, a smile on his face, and a tattoo on his arm.

In all my years of ministry, I have never seen anybody as sold out and excited about a ministry as Gary Phipps. When he heard about Lifewise, he researched it wholeheartedly and went all in. He eats, sleeps, and breathes Lifewise. When you talk about the little children that are hearing about Jesus, he lights up like a Christmas tree. His hat, his tee-shirt, and his sweatshirt all have the Lifewise logo on them, and if we could see his heart, there would be a tattoo of Lifewise on it. He not only talks about the vision, he also works on the vision. He is helping to spread it to surrounding counties, states, and I'm sure, eventually to the world. Lord, give us a fiery zeal for your vision like Gary.

To keep the visionary fire hot, you must stoke its flames. As a teenage boy on the farm it was my job to bring the firewood into the house for the night. So often we would have only unseasoned wood. It was green and wet, so it didn't burn hot unless you added a little coal. The coal burned hot, therefore the wood dried quicker and burned hotter. The moral of the story is to spend valuable time with people who are full of the Spirit, strong in the Word, and live hot for Jesus. It's been said many times that in ten years you will be the product of who you spend time with, the books you read, and the places you have been.

COMMUNICATE THE VISION

Vision is ignited in the heart of the followers by communication. The vision will be stillborn if it is not communicated in word, deed, attitude, and passion. When people refuse to follow, usually it's because they don't understand. Keep talking. Share the why and the how and keep on sharing. One Nehemiah principle is to repeat the vision every 30 days because people forget the why. Encourage people to ask questions. Be a good listener and you will answer the questions correctly. There are times we are answering questions nobody is asking. A good communicator is one who is so full of vision that when they open their mouth, knowledge flows out like a river at flood stage.

You can't communicate something you are not sold on yourself. If there is any doubt or uncertainty in you it will be detected. When there is poor communication, you find the pastor headed in one direction and the leaders going in another. The gulf widens each day that the vision is not communicated. Conversely, there is great strength produced when we take the time to talk about the vision. Be confident, bold, and full of faith. Share the vision every chance you get. Share with staff members, boards, small groups, and from the pulpit.

Communication requires a team of influencers. One person cannot pull the wagon to the top of the hill himself. The pastor visionary must surround himself with people of influence. The pastor must multiply his voice through others. Any time spent with them is well-invested time. John Maxwell said, "People will buy into the leader before they will buy into the vision."[31] Charlie McCloud, a founding elder of Cornerstone has told me many times, "I am here because I believe in you." Charlie is one of the most influential voices of the vision because of our relationship. We meet monthly to talk about the vision. When there is a breakdown of communication, there is an invisible wall that begins to form. The enemy injects lies, doubts, and suspicion into people's minds. Good communication keeps the line of vision clear.

I also meet weekly with my pastoral staff. As we communicate openly about the vision of Cornerstone Church, the Lord is able to expand and enhance the vision. It enables us to all stay on track and not to veer off course. When lines of communication break down, the vision is no longer clear. People wander without a clear vision. So often people will develop their own vision based on what they want it to be. Communication of God's vision will help avoid many pitfalls and advance the Kingdom of God.

Nehemiah saw the importance of casting vision, "You see the trouble we are in: Jerusalem lies in ruins, and its gates have been burned with fire. Come, let us rebuild the wall of

Jerusalem, and we will no longer be in disgrace" (Nehemiah 2:17 NIV). How often do we need to recast vision? Israel got discouraged and stopped rebuilding the wall. Nehemiah had to recast the vision. I'm a firm believer in keeping the vision before God's people. That's because people are quick to forget why and what they are doing. Nehemiah's plan was genius and palatable for the people to follow: just rebuild the wall in front of your own house. Every day each family stared at the wall and was reminded of the vision.

Keep talking. Look for creative ways to communicate with your leaders. You should show genuine interest in them. Asking them about their family or their newborn are easy conversation starters. When communication is lacking there is an invisible wall that forms and the vision is unclear.

When we fail to communicate the vision people are uncertain of where they are going. It is difficult for people to follow if they don't know where they are going. Good leaders map out the vision and show the people a clear path that will get them to their destination of purposeful vision. When people see clearly, they are more apt to accept and follow the vision.

BE A SKILLFUL CASTER

A dear lifetime friend of mine, Bob Samson, was a fisherman. As he grew older and his body began to break down, I sought opportunities to spend some quality time with him. Even though I had little interest in fishing, I asked him to take me fishing. He gladly accepted my request and we set a date. Now Bob was not an occasional fisherman, he was an avid fisherman. Bob was retired but still painted professionally when he wasn't fishing. He told me that all of his painting money went to fishing equipment. I was amazed at the amount of fishing supplies he had in his basement. One entire room was dedicated just to his hobby. There was enough to start his own store.

The time arrived and we headed to Seneca Lake to fish for crappie. Bob had started from scratch with me, teaching me how to bait the hook and everything about fishing. I had never taken a hook out of a fish's mouth but wanted to learn quickly. No way did I want anybody to see Bob have to do that for me. It came time to cast our lines into the water. Bob was a good teacher, and I caught on quickly. I never snagged anybody around me with my hook. There were several people fishing near us on the shore, but Bob was the only one catching fish. Total strangers were looking to see what kind of bait Bob was using. Young men who could have been our grandsons were baffled as to Bob's success. Some were brave enough to ask and Bob gladly told them. It was a combination of the right bait and the place to cast. You see you can have the best rod and reel and even the proper bait, but if you don't know where the fish are, you're not going to catch fish. You can also know where the fish are but if you are using the wrong bait, the fish won't bite.

Casting vision requires skill and experience. You have to know your people. You can't force anything on people, they won't bite. The vision has to look appealing to the people and the people have to be hungry. Prayer is the first step in vision casting. Prayer will create a hunger for God-ordained vision in the hearts of God's people. Through prayer the visionary receives the vision and through prayer he delivers the vision. The bait is attractive because it is the gospel of Jesus Christ. The vision is actually Christ and His mission. He came to seek and save the lost. Any vision that is not centered on the ministry of winning souls and discipling believers is not the vision of Christ.

Many fishermen only fish for the big one. They are passionate about catching that wall hanger. I liken the wall hanger to the person you win to Christ that God uses to be a great influencer in the kingdom. Maybe they become a minister, pastor, missionary, or a businessman that touches hundreds and even thousands with the gospel. Stanley Tam was the CEO of U.S. Plastic who God used to win many souls to the Lord. His autobiography is called God Owns My Business. Every Christian should not only fish for the big one but all kinds and sizes of fish. You never know how God is going to use that next soul. I have seen what I thought was a person of little talent grow into a successful minister of the gospel.

You must understand that although I am not a fisherman, I have heard many fishermen declare the fish are not biting because it is too hot. Many will fish early in the morning or late evening. Timing is everything if you're going to cast your line into the water and expect to catch fish.

Timing is everything to vision casting. You never cast vision when a church has gone through a time of crisis. That's the time to comfort the people. You would never cast a vision to build a new sanctuary if the church just suffered from a church split. When the church is healthy and full of hope and expectancy, that is a good time to cast vision. When you have new gifted people ready for leadership, it may be time to launch that new ministry you have prayed about for years.

The anointing of the Holy Spirit sets the hook. He is the One that seals the deal. The Spirit gives wisdom to properly draw a picture of the vision God has given you. You receive it by the Holy Spirit and deliver it by the Holy Spirit. You can be the best salesperson, but it is the Holy Spirit that witnesses to people's hearts that this is God speaking to them. Ask God to anoint you to cast His vision. Do your homework but trust completely in Him.

CASTING TAKES COMMITMENT

Paul the Apostle was a man that modeled commitment to Christ. His entire life was a testament of true Biblical commitment. His message was total commitment to his followers. It was all or nothing: get in, get out, or get run over. Paul writes to Timothy, "Thou therefore, my son, be strong in the grace that is in Christ Jesus. And the things that thou has heard of me among many witnesses, the same commit thou to faithful men, who shall be able to teach others also" (2 Timothy 2:1-2).

In order to cast vision, one must be wholeheartedly committed to the vision. Maxie Dunham tells us, "The danger I feel is a cynicism in those who do the job well but without a do-or-die commitment like every forward-moving kingdom enterprise deserves and demands."[32]

I heard the testimony of a church that had hired a long line of preachers. Every time, just as the congregation grew to love them, the preacher would resign and move on to what he thought was a better opportunity in ministry. A new minister was hired, and he struggled to get close to the people. He tried and tried to no avail, but it seemed there was a barrier he couldn't penetrate. Finally, the head of the church asked him when he was going to leave them. The people shared with the new pastor their hurts and fears that he too would leave them. He tried to reassure them but was unsuccessful. He went home and told his wife his discovery. The couple agreed they would have to do something to convince the congregation they were planning on staying for their lifetime. After much prayer, they had an idea. They went to the local funeral director and purchased grave plots for both of them. That next Sunday they showed the congregation the deeds to their grave plots and reassured them they were committed to them for life. The wall came down when the congregation saw the couple's commitment. That's the type of commitment it takes to be a vision caster. Some people will watch for months and even years to see how committed you are. Maybe they have had preachers break their hearts in the past. These people will eventually come around when others begin to follow the vision.

I would be the first one to tell you that I struggled with commitment before I came to know Christ. I had never seen commitment in my childhood or family. My wife was the most committed person I had ever met. As much as I loved that quality in her, it was still a struggle. My only commitment was to me. When I surrendered my life to Christ, He taught me commitment. Instantly, commitment became one of my strongest character traits. After all that Jesus had done for me, how could I hold anything back from Him? Casting vision is not easy. That's why there cannot be a lack of commitment to the cause. Spend time with people who are committed. It tends to rub off on you. What may have been a weakness can and will become a strength. I encourage you to read about successful vision casters. They all share the same never-ending, never waning, passionate commitment to Christ's vision.

One of the most inspiring statements of faith comes from the "Prayer of a Martyred Zimbabwe Pastor:"

"I am part of the fellowship of the unashamed. I have the Holy Spirit power. The die has been cast. I have stepped over the line. The decision has been made – I'm a disciple of His. I won't look back, let up, slow down, back away, or be still. My past is redeemed, my present makes sense, my future is secure. I'm finished and done with low living, sight walking, smooth knees, colorless dreams, tamed vision, worldly talking, cheap giving, and dwarfed goals. I no longer need preeminence, prosperity, position, promotions, plaudits, or popularity. I don't have to be right, first, tops, recognized, praised, regarded or rewarded. I now live by faith, lean in His presence, walk by patience, am uplifted by prayers, and I labor with power. My face is set, my gait is fast, my goal is heaven, my road is narrow, my way rough, my companions are few, my Guide reliable, my mission clear. I cannot be bought, compromised, detoured, lured away, turned back, deluded, delayed. I will not flinch in the face of sacrifice, hesitate in the presence of the enemy, pander in the pool of popularity, or meander in the maze of mediocrity. I won't give up, shut up, let up, until I have stayed, stored up, prayed up, paid up, preached up for the cause of Christ. I am a disciple of Jesus. I must go till He comes, give till I drop, preach till all know, and work till He stops me. And, when He comes for His own, He will have no problem recognizing me...my banner will be clear."[33]

There are many methods of vision casting in pioneering a church. Every one of them has its weaknesses and strengths. They all require much work and perseverance.

CASTING VISION REQUIRES PERSEVERANCE

According to Wikipedia, the "father of modern missions" was William Carey. He joined the Baptist missionaries in 1793 and moved to Calcutta, India. Carey opened a school for needy children and later the first theological university. He was the embodiment of perseverance preaching faithfully the gospel of Jesus Christ for seven years before winning his first convert.

With every vision there will be opposition and discouraging times. It has been said, "Winners never quit and quitters never win." We must run to the finish line. If there is an ounce of quit in you, it will outweigh the whole vision and you will eventually stop. When we put our heart and soul into the vision, nothing will stop us. Like Paul the Apostle states in Acts 20:24, "None of these things move me." Just like a tree planted by the water, I shall not be moved.

Every great man or woman of God must count the cost by asking if he or she is willing to give it their all to see the vision fulfilled. In Genesis 6-8, Noah received a vision from God to build an Ark to save his family and the whole human race. The price was high, but he took ownership.

He cast the vision to his sons, and they bought into the vision as well. It took Noah and his sons one hundred years to complete the Ark. He never quit preaching and warning the people of judgment to come, yet he gained not one convert. You talk about perseverance; Noah is the man. Only God knows all the blisters, pulled muscles, broken bones, sweat, blood, and tears. Think of all the songs of ridicule that must have been sung to the faithful family. Noah fought through doubts and fears, having never seen rain, much less a flood. But the vision propelled him on to that day when the animals were loaded on board and God shut the door of the Ark. The unseen Hand of God they had felt strengthening them for all those years then reached down and closed the door and the first raindrop fell. The mighty deluge would lift the boat. The Ark would sit on dry land 150 days later. Noah must have breathed a sigh of relief when he, his family and all the animals stepped off the Ark after a full year of confinement. When we stretch ourselves and persevere, God supernaturally shows up to fulfill the vision. As the saying goes: "Visions are caught, not taught." Catch the vision.

ATTRACTIVE VISION

CHAPTER TEN

A few years ago, a dear friend of mine, James McDonald, told me of the impact the commercials our church produced in the early 90s had on his life. He said when he felt many churches in our area had lost touch with the needs of people, we came along speaking life, hope, and joy into our community. The vision of genuine loving and caring for people seemed to be refreshing to him. We simply interviewed people in our church asking them what Cornerstone Church meant to them. For several years, we aired those testimonies on WHIZ-TV. The response was very positive. People like James were encouraged to seek God with their whole heart and renew their commitment to Him. This is what I call attractive vision. You see, people don't care how much you know until they know how much you care. People just want to see Jesus. Dead, dull religion is a turn-off to everybody. Attractive vision presents Jesus to people in a way that draws people to Him: "I am come that they might have life, and that they might have it more abundantly" (John 10:10b). This is life that overflows with joy, peace, and purpose. Religion is man's quest for God where relationship is knowing Him personally. When Jesus is presented as who He really is and what He is really like, people run to Him. As Christ's ambassadors, it is our job to show the world the beauty of the

Lord and then they will be attracted to Him. May our vision be so Christ-centered that people will only see Jesus.

GENUINE LOVE

The greatest testimony of a church is that the people are loving and welcoming. We hear that statement constantly from first-time guests and new people at Cornerstone. Everybody wants to be loved. Our motto since we started the church in 1986 has been "Everybody is somebody at Cornerstone." There are no big "I's" and little "you's" at Cornerstone. We teach and practice love. Paul the Apostle said in 1 Corinthians 13:13b (NLT), "And the greatest of these is love." It's one thing to talk about it, but it is another thing to walk in love at all times. Pastor Troy Ervin and I were talking about practicing love in the church. I confessed to him that years ago I was under a lot of stress with building projects at the church. During a church banquet at The Barracks Youth Center the place was full. While I was trying to eat people kept stopping to talk to me. I put on a smile but found myself annoyed. I thought why don't people leave me alone? No doubt people could see I didn't want to be bothered. Later when the Holy Spirit began to convict me about my thoughts, repentance flowed from my lips. How had I become so insensitive to good loving people? My eating habits would need to change. Now, feeding on the valuable love and fellowship while others are eating is my protocol. At times, Pat will have to say, "Steve, sit down here and eat." I'll never forget the lesson learned. Loving people and showing that love is far more important than a meal. Pastor Troy came up with a brilliant idea. He said you should write a book and entitle it, "What's Love Got to Do with It?" We laughed and acknowledged love has everything to do with it.

People just want to be loved. Women, men, boys, and girls all need to feel loved. For some people the only time they feel loved is at church. If you love somebody, tell them. You can't tell them when they are gone. At first, some people, especially men, don't know how to respond when you tell them you love them. It makes me smile within when eventually they will return the sentiment.

We are living in a day where true love has grown cold. Jesus said in Matthew 24:12, "And because iniquity shall abound, the love of many shall wax cold." At this time in a self-centered, narcissistic culture, we the church need to rebrand ourselves. The church has become known for what we stand against more than for what we stand for: "But speaking the truth in love, may grow up into him in all things, which is the head, even Christ" (Ephesians 4:15). We can speak the truth in love without compromising. In our culture, we are told you don't love me if you don't agree with me. Real love tells the truth in love. Jesus loved the Pharisees enough to tell them the truth. He told the woman at the well the truth in love. Erase all doubts in people's minds and tell them you love them.

It is love that is attractive to unsaved people. When they see the church in action, loving one another with open arms and welcoming them into the family, they come running. When people step into the foyer at Cornerstone Church, greeters open the door for them. The next person hands them a bulletin and the next opens the door into the sanctuary and greets them with a smile. If people have any questions, in the middle of the foyer is the "Connect Desk," with smiling, helpful people waiting to be of service. When people are seated, C12 leaders, pastors, and other leaders are going throughout the sanctuary greeting people. Friendly, loving churches do not get there by accident; they are trained. It starts at the top with leadership setting the standard. Pastors have to be approachable, friendly, and loving at all times. People are never a bother. We are there to serve them. You have heard the statement like father, like son. In the church: like pastor, like congregation. Love is modeled by leadership. It is contagious. "But by love serve one another" (Galatians 5:13b).

When first-time guests visit Cornerstone, we want to make them feel welcome, loved, and important. After our worship time, we ask first-time guests to raise their hands. We welcome them with a round of applause. The ushers give them a first-time guest card to fill out and turn it into the Connect Desk and receive their gift bag. That week the pastor sends each person a hand-written letter welcoming them to the church family. They receive a phone call from one of the pastors and a loaf of freshly baked bread is delivered to their home. Word got around about the bread. When somebody receives a loaf of bread they tell other people how good it and the church are. We are so glad people feel loved. All of this helps people to see our heart and they begin trusting us. We can then begin the discipleship process with them. We want people to have a good foundation of faith.

When you genuinely love people it shows. Jesus' life and ministry was based on love. He loved the lowest of sinners, the extremely poor, and even the rich. To the rich young ruler in Mark 10:21-22, Jesus expressed his love by inviting him to follow Him. In verse 21 it says, "Then Jesus beholding him loved him." Jesus loved him enough to call him out of sin and offer him eternal life. May we always love like Jesus loves.

Love is the true motivation for the church. Any other motive will short-circuit the vision. If love is missing from the vision the church will cease to be attractive to both church members and outsiders. People cannot be forced into loving each other. A greater commitment by leaders won't do. It takes compassion. The Spirit inspired loving compassion of the community of God's people will win conversions.

A good friend of mine accepted his first pastoral role. He was young and lacked experience. The church was small, and frustration eventually set in. Instead of reaching out to older ministers for advice and encouragement, he began to scold the church. It was their fault the church was not growing, he told them. He created an unpleasant environment and eventually was dismissed. I have always said that if you want to build a church make sure people feel better when they leave than when they came. They will want to come back and bring somebody with them. Love has everything to do with it!

PEOPLE ARE THE CHURCH'S GREATEST COMMODITY

People are the church's main treasure. We should cherish people. Live, love, and laugh with them. Listen to their fears, failures, and feelings. Rejoice when they win and encourage them when they fall. Jesus died for people; we must value them as highly as Jesus does.

Paul the Apostle refers to the church as His body, His workmanship, His household, His holy temple, His bride, and His army in the book of Ephesians. All of these titles present the workings of God's people. Without people, there is no church. The minister must realize how valuable people are and show them. It has been said that the sheep just need the shepherd to pet them once in a while. A good shepherd smells like sheep. He takes time for the sheep. Someone else can say the same thing but, it doesn't heal like when the shepherd says it. Shepherds that don't like sheep are in the wrong business. They will do more harm than good.

A lady at church approached me after the service was over. She needed to talk (she really needed a counseling session) and all I could see was a line of people waiting to talk to me. I was distracted and kept looking at the line. She moved around in front of me to block my view of other people and then said, "Okay, now I have your attention." I learned some valuable lessons that day. First of all, give people your undivided attention; they deserve it. Second, ask the person to give you a minute to greet people and then sit down and talk or schedule a counseling session. Third, don't let the same person occupy all of your time after every service.

All genuine leaders excel in happy, wholesome relationships. Excellent relationships among staff members are the raw materials of a happy, productive team. Look for staff personnel who love people and show it. In the Cornerstone School of

Ministry, I teach about the reasons people no longer frequent a business or a church. The first reason is that 1% of people die. Second, 3% move. Third, 5% quit because of a friend. Fourth, 9% find better pricing. Fifth, 14% are not satisfied with the product. Finally, 68% leave because of a poor, unfriendly attitude.

Few people will put up with an abusive, bad attitude. Every leader or worker in your church should check his or her attitude periodically. Ask others: "How am I presenting myself?" People are drawn to pleasant, personable people. Not only is it important to care for new people attending a church, but it is equally as important to care for long-time members. If a member is going through a crisis they need pastoral support. "Rejoice with them that do rejoice, and weep with them that weep" (Romans 12:15). When church members lose loved ones, it is important to be there for them as much as possible. Flowers always say we love you and care. A phone call, a card, a visit, or a meal always fit the occasion. Attractive vision cares about hurting people. You don't serve for a pat on the back. Blessed people who have their needs met will tell others. Every good deed is a stroke of the brush on the portrait of an attractive vision that glorifies the Lord and builds confidence in people.

Our motto at Cornerstone is "Love God – Love People." You can't love one and not the other. It takes both. It is the love of God that teaches us how to love people. If you are struggling to love someone, ask the Father to love them through you. His love is supernatural. If He loves us in spite of all of our sins, He can empower us to love the unlovable. 1 John 4:16-20 reinforces this love,

"And we have known and believed the love that God hath to us. God is love; and he that dwelleth in love dwelleth in God, and God in him. Herein is our love made perfect, that we may have boldness in the Day of Judgment: because as He is, so are we in this world. There is no fear in love; but perfect love casteth out fear: because fear hath torment. He that feareth is not made perfect in love. We love Him, because He first loved us. If any man say, I love God, and hateth his brother, he is a liar: for he that loveth not his brother whom he hath seen, how can he love God whom he hath not seen."

EXCELLENCE IS ATTRACTIVE

The sharing of the gospel is the most important thing that takes place here on earth. In every way we share, it should be done with excellence. Some people have the mindset that it's good enough for the church. Only excellence is good enough for the church because the church is Christ's and He is worthy of our best.

Let's start with God's house. When Israel returned from the Exile, God chastised them because they had rebuilt their homes but failed to rebuild God's house. He told them they would put clothes on, but they would not be warm, they would earn wages and put them in bags with holes in them. He called a drought upon the land of their prosperity. The Lord stirred up Zerubbabel to motivate the people. The people responded correctly. They came and rebuilt the house of the Lord (See

Haggai Chapter 1).

I have always believed the house of the Lord should be clean. It should be updated when necessary. The remodeling and updating is never over at Cornerstone. We want the facilities to look and function nicely for God's glory. We want the sound system and lighting to be state-of- the-art. God is a God of excellence. Look at the Temples, the Tabernacle, and even the design of the Ark; they were all built with excellence. In Revelation Chapter 21, we read about the beauty of the New Heaven. Walls of jasper, gates of pearls, streets of gold, and even the foundation is made of precious stones. Take pride in God's house. We don't worship the house, but it is a tool we use for God's glory. Build it and maintain it with excellence.

Attractive vision is clearly seen in the lives of people. The way they live a life of holiness, honesty, and integrity reflects the teaching and preaching that is presented week in and week out. People learn best when there is a consistent leader or leaders who reflect the image of Christ. We live in an age where many are departing from the faith. 1 Timothy 4:1 warns of such departure: "Now the Spirit speaketh expressly, that in the latter times some shall depart from the faith, giving heed to seducing spirits, and doctrines of devils." The Amplified Bible adds, "doctrines that demons teach." Many preachers are compromising the Word of God, no longer warning people of eternal punishment for the wicked. They are calling good evil and evil good. They have abandoned the Word of God and embraced the lies of the devil. Where there is no standard there is no Christianity.

Years ago, a person who attends Cornerstone Church and

lives in Morgan County told me what they heard that people were saying about the church. They referred to it as the church that preaches against alcohol consumption. God's Word is very clear about drunkenness. 1 Corinthians 6:10, "nor thieves, nor covetous, nor drunkards, nor revilers, nor extortioners, shall inherit the Kingdom of God." There is great debate concerning how many is too many. Though I do not condemn others, my answer is abstinence. You will never have to worry about being an alcoholic or alcohol being a gateway to drugs or more destructive drugs if you abstain.

New Age teachings have crept into the church. Preachers tell people that everybody is going to heaven. Whatever happened to Jesus' teaching on the straight and narrow way? Matthew 7:13- 14 says, "Enter ye in at the strait gate: for wide is the gate, and broad is the way, that leadeth to destruction, and many there be which go in thereat: because strait is the gate, and narrow is the way, which leadeth unto life, and few there be that find it."

I have discovered that most people want the truth. True seekers want the whole truth, nothing but the truth. "And ye shall know the truth, and the truth shall make you free" (John 8:32). Be a lover of truth and a hater of lies. Hate what God hates. "The fear of the Lord is to hate evil: pride, and arrogancy, and the evil way, and the froward mouth, do I hate" (Proverbs 8:13). Truth seekers stand under the authority of the Word of God. The Lord requires clean hands and honest hearts for His work.

This century, along with all other centuries, is sex crazy. The thing that makes this age so much more dangerous is the availability of pornography. It is a scourge to our society and clergy today. In the U.S.A., the porn industry generates between $10 billion to $15 billion a year. Even ministers are vulnerable to satanic attacks of lust when they do not stay full of the Holy Spirit. We must guard our hearts and minds proclaiming as David said in Psalm 101:3, "I will set no wicked thing before mine eyes: I hate the work of them that turn aside." There are multiple resources for those who are bound by the sin of pornography. True repentance will change the way you act and think. Seek out an accountability person to help you. Don't be another statistic of a minister or man who has lost his ministry or his family. Today women are just as vulnerable as men. Keep your guard up and your eyes where they belong. Attractive ministry is pure and holy.

Excellence in ministry requires discipline. Paul was a disciplined man who accomplished great things for the Kingdom of God. "And every man that striveth for the mastery is temperate in all things... but I keep under my body, and bring it into subjection: lest that by all means, when I have preached to others, I myself should be a castaway" (1 Corinthians 9:25, 27). Discipline puts us in a position to hear from God. Being well-prepared going into Sunday enables the Holy Spirit to use us. Be prayed up and full of the Word He has given you. This will set the stage for God to move.

Be rested up and give God your best, and He will give you His best. People have always responded enthusiastically to the best. In the Old Testament, the Queen of Sheba traveled hundreds of miles to see Solomon's ministry of excellence. In the New Testament, Jesus healed a deaf and dumb man: "And the people were beyond measure astonished, saying, He hath done all things well: He maketh both the deaf to hear, and the dumb to speak" (Mark 7:32- 37). Jesus did all things excellently then and He wants to now through us. Be the ministry others want to come to visit and see what God is doing. Jesus is the same yesterday, today, and forever (See Hebrews 13:8). He wants to work His wonders through His children. The excellence of ministry that is attractive is led by and empowered by the Holy Spirit.

ENCOURAGEMENT IS ATTRACTIVE MINISTRY

Not long ago, I told a young believer I was proud of him. He replied, "Thank you, that means a lot to me." He has only been saved about two years and is serving on the Safety Team at church. Never underestimate the positive effect a word of encouragement might have on a person. Everybody needs to hear an affirming word now and then. It boosts your spirit and drives the lies of the devil down the road. The "V.O.J." – Voice of Judgment – doesn't have a chance when encouragement steps up to the plate.

Years ago, Mark Pfeifer gave me a nickname. He said you are a Barnabas. Instantly I was blessed because I knew what the name Barnabas means. It means "Son of Encouragement" (Acts 4:36-37 AMP). Barnabas sold land and gave it to the apostles to distribute it to the needy Christians in Jerusalem. He also took John Mark under his wing when he had failed in ministry. An encourager will not give up on people. They see the best in people and are willing to walk the road to restoration with them (See Acts 15:37-39).

One day while working at the Ohio Ferro Alloy some of my old friends began to tease me and I chose to walk away. An older man walked up to me, put his hand on my shoulder and said, "I'm proud of you. You are on the right track. Don't listen to those guys." That was about 48 years ago, and I still feel the power of those encouraging words.

A man recently began attending Cornerstone Church. After a short time, he told me, "Cornerstone's reputation has preceded itself." He said, "I have heard this church was an encouraging place and now I have experienced it firsthand." God's love and power, with a lot of human encouragement, is changing him little by little.

I appreciate all the modern technology the Lord has given us at Cornerstone, but what attracts people week after week to worship with us is the abiding Presence of God. He is with us and working through us. May we ever follow this chapter's title and be an *Attractive Vision* for Jesus.

THE SYNERGY OF VISION

CHAPTER ELEVEN

Vision is only as effective as the synergy among the visionary team. Synergy means "the working together of two things to produce an effect greater than the sum of their individual effects."[34] It is a fact that every time you add a helper to the group your production increases exponentially. Whether you add a worker to the carpentry crew or to the ministry team you increase production at a greater rate.

A good example of synergy on the farm took place when we were planning on installing French drains in the pasture field. The first step was to call all underground utility companies to have the location checked for underground utilities. When the field representative arrived, he realized it would require a lot of walking to locate and mark the gas line. I offered to drive him back and forth on my side-by-side as he placed the line locators. Working together it didn't take us long to locate the lines and get the job done. It saved much time and caused less stress on his sore knees.

Learning to work together takes time. The old saying, "teamwork makes the dream work" is so true. Everybody approaches work a little differently. We all have strengths and weaknesses. When we acknowledge that we need each other, we can learn so much from each other. Hard-headedness teaches nothing and gets little done. There is so much value in teamwork. The possibilities are endless when we work together. It is a beautiful sight to behold when churches work together in a community. The Kingdom of God is advanced, and the world sees true Christianity in action. Here in Muskingum County, many churches work together. During the Christmas season the Salvation Army raises money for the needy through its Red Kettle Campaign. Many people from local churches volunteer to make the mission a success. The Global Methodist Church in Chandlersville presents a live nativity every year at Thanksgiving called the Bethlehem Walk. It takes a lot of work, but people from many churches work together to bless hundreds of people yearly. At Cornerstone Church, during the Easter season, we produce the musical drama Worthy is the Lamb. Over 120 people work together in the cast with some of them from other churches. It is such a joy to see the body of Christ work together as a family. I'm sure it pleases our Heavenly Father. One or two people cannot accomplish great things for God, but a team with good leadership can do anything. All things are possible with God when His children work together in unity. As the Bible puts it, "Behold, how good and how pleasant it is for brethren to dwell together in unity" (Psalm 133:1)! And it also says, "Two are better than one; because they have a good reward for their labour" (Ecclesiastes 4:9).

The miraculous effects of synergy are not only seen in God's church, but they also work for the world as well. After Noah built the Ark and saved mankind from the flood, God commanded him to replenish the earth. Some people refused and wanted to huddle up, build a city, a tower, and make a name for themselves. In Genesis chapter 11 we see rebellious people making bricks and declaring they would build a tower reaching to heaven. Their plans were to build a city for themselves. In verses five and six, "And the Lord came down to see the city and the tower, which the children of men builded. And the Lord said, behold the people is one, and they have all one language; and this they begin to do; and now nothing will be restrained from them, which they have imagined to do." God had to confound their language to scatter them. Even though they were in defiant rebellion, the power of synergy worked for them until God stepped in and stopped them.

I love teamwork and if used correctly the Lord loves teamwork. We can accomplish so much good for God when we work together. When people refuse to work together the Kingdom of God is greatly hindered. I am Kingdom-minded. In order to be, you can't be selfish or self-seeking. Mike Murdock, a great teacher of the gospel said, "What you make happen for others, God will make happen for you." I love working with people no matter who does the leading – just so God gets the glory.

WORK IN SYNERGY

I love to work. It is a part of my DNA. It's who I am. Work is a four-letter word God not only permits but encourages. In the Garden of Eden, there was work to do in caring for the garden. The Lord said to Adam, "This is your job. Take good care of the beautiful place I have given you to live." Everybody needs a job to do in God's Kingdom. It wasn't long before Adam and Eve had two sons. One was a tiller of the ground and the other raised sheep. Both were taught to work with responsibility. There was a division that formed between the boys when they failed to work together. Jealousy set in to Cain's heart and he killed his brother, Abel. I wonder what would have happened if they had worked together.

The number one element in ministry is trust. Trust will hold a church, family, or business together. A lack of trust allows jealousy and hate to creep into a relationship. The outcome is disastrous. Pride is one of the biggest downfalls of many ministers and lay people. It's been said, the greatest form of humility is to ask. To ask for help is a sign of strength, not weakness.

Recently, in our weekly ministers meeting, one of the pastors opened up about his struggle with burnout. I was somewhat surprised because he always looked like everything was fine. I was so proud of him for the fact that he didn't put on his smiley face and act like everything was fine.

So many people, especially men, find it hard to admit they are human and hurt at times. We tend to fake it until we can make it, which is very dangerous. The ministers gathered around him for prayer and words of encouragement. There is nothing like love, encouragement, and support when you are discouraged. He told us he was going to take a sabbatical. We all agreed that was a wise decision and offered any means of help or support.

As a young man, I found it hard to ask for help. My back

had to be against the wall before I would ask. It was pride that kept me from asking. Most people want to help when somebody is in need - if they just ask. I have also noticed the people at church love to help. When people are asked to help, it makes them feel needed. "Yet ye have not, because ye ask not" (James 4:2b). Everybody wins when you ask. You get help and the helper walks away feeling they have worth and something to offer. They feel a sense of ownership and appreciation. They will serve with a smile on their face.

On a side note, we always make sure there is something to eat if people are going to be serving long. Men especially appreciate it. The way to a man's heart is through his stomach. If you're going to work the ox you have to feed them.

Building a great church or a successful business takes rolling up your sleeves and going to work. I like what one politician said during a campaign, "He might have more money than me to spend on advertising, but I will outwork him." Hard work never hurts anybody, but it can help everybody when channeled in the right direction. Many people want everything handed to them on a silver platter. That's our culture. I still believe there are no free lunches. Somebody paid for that meal. Thank God for those who will sacrifice for those in need, but so many take advantage of good, giving people today. People that always receive handouts miss out on the joy and satisfaction of working hard. They also miss out on the joy of being a giver. For 38 years I have watched Cornerstone Church maintain the reputation of a hard-working church. We have risen to the challenge of building buildings and building lives. It is hard work driving nails, but even harder work hammering out the problems that face so many people. God blesses those who work hard in whatever capacity to build His Kingdom. You win with good, salt of the earth people. Rather than complaining, put on your servant's apron and go to work.

I am so blessed to have good friends like Mike and Cathy Bullock. They have always been hard workers. They pioneered Hands of Faith Church in the early 90's. Through all of their ups and downs, triumphs and pain they have remained steady and diligent. The biggest trial they have gone through is the passing of their grandson, Miles. They transformed their pain into purpose and began Miles' Mission. There is a redemptive purpose the Bullock family has discovered in their pain. Now they are taking their message of hope to the hurting all across the USA.

Hard work definitely pays off and impacts people. Years ago, we were building a Christian Camp with three dormitory buildings that included a shower house attached to one of the buildings. It was a Saturday morning and about 35 church members were working on the buildings. I noticed a car drive up the lane and stop behind me. When I looked around, I saw a local businessman with a big smile on his face. I went over to talk to him to see what he wanted. Before I could ask, his eyes filled with tears and he said, "Look at all these people." He repeated himself, "Look at all of these people, working together for a common goal." He couldn't get over all of those people volunteering their time and talents to build the camp. That day I believe his faith in mankind and the Lord was renewed. Think of what Nehemiah said about the children of Israel as they worked to rebuild the wall around Jerusalem: "For the people had a mind to work" (Nehemiah 4:6b).

So often we make decisions without adequately preparing to follow through. That's why Solomon said in Ecclesiastes 7:8, "Better is the end of a thing than the beginning thereof..." It's easy to celebrate when you begin a project, but to complete the task might take years of consistent labor and toil. Much sweat, blood, and tears are the high cost of the hard work of vision. Jesus warns that we must count the cost before we profess to be followers of Him (See Luke 14:27-33). One of my favorite pastors and authors was Jack Hyles who said, "I learned that great works do not just happen. They are caused." This is like someone building a structure, they must count the cost to see if there are sufficient funds.

SYNERGY IN CRISIS

Crisis has a way of driving good people together. When our granddaughter Laikyn Ashley Wisecarver died of an accidental overdose after being clean for 13 months, our family was devastated. She was a beautiful 27-year-old full of life and personality. Her laugh was infectious and contagious. I told my wife that we would make it through this together. My lovely daughter Jodi Niceswanger, Laikyn's mother, has chosen to take this crisis and use it to help others. She started an outreach to help break barriers and to give hope to those currently in recovery or beginning their recovery journey, called Laikyn's Legacy of Hope. Many have chosen recovery and have been helped because of it. Crisis has drawn us closer together as a family. It has also caused us to deepen our commitment to Christ. We have chosen to cling to the old rugged cross and our Savior who died on that cross for us.

There is a reason God tells us to count it all joy when we fall into diverse temptations. He said the trying of our faith worketh patience. Trials will expose our weak links. At that time, the Lord makes our weak links our point of greatest strength. "My brethren, count it all joy when ye fall into divers temptations; knowing this, that the trying of your faith worketh patience. But let patience have her perfect work, that ye may be perfect and entire, wanting nothing" (James 1:2- 4).

It is the Lord's strength that enables us to develop patience in the time of devastating crises. It's at those times we are encouraged to pray and ask for wisdom (See James 1:5). God's wisdom and power are multiplied in the synergy of prayer. After James was killed by the sword at Herod's command, the king next decided to kill Peter after Easter (See Acts 12:2-5). He waited too long because the church began to pray constantly. Simon Peter was held in shackles between two armed guards. It amazes me how he was able to sleep knowing Herod's plans to kill him. The same God that gave Daniel peace between those lions in that den of lions is the same God that gave Simon Peter peace. Peter's intervention was due to the unified prayer of the church. One angel dispatched to Peter's rescue took care of the job. He first had to wake him up. The angel kicked Peter in the side and told him to get up and get dressed. There was no need for a lantern because of the brightness of the angel. He said, "Follow me." As they approached each gate, it opened on its own. Still, Peter thought this was a vision until the last gate slammed shut. Then he realized he was free. Evidently, he knew of the prayer meeting at John Mark's mother's house because he went straight there. The whole prayer meeting thought he was an angel. Just like many believers, when God answers their prayers, they say, "I can't believe that." Really? You believed in prayer and now you can't believe? As the old worship song says, "Only believe, only believe all things are possible, only believe." When you are facing times of crisis call upon the intercessors that know how to pray the matter through. Watch the shackles fall off and the barriers be removed. Stand in the gap for others, and somebody will stand in the gap for you when in crisis. We are most like Jesus when we truly care enough to pray or even reach out a helping hand. There is wonder-working power in united prayer. Look what took place on the day of Pentecost. One hundred twenty people became of one mind and one accord, and heaven came down. The Holy Spirit gave birth and power to the infant church (See Acts 2:1-4).

When we are united in the synergy of vision, no task is too small. "For who hath despised the day of small things" (Zechariah 4:10)? The Lord started with two souls, Adam and Eve, and told them to replenish the earth. He could have made a thousand just as easily, but God knows the possibility of seed faith. There is no limit. He started over with Noah and his family, eight in all. He started with Jesus and his 12 disciples and through them took the gospel to the world. Some people only think about big numbers. Start where the Lord plants you. Little is much if the Lord is in it.

Wherever He plants me I will be content to grow, it's all about Him not my little show. Like the giant sequoia trees that draw their strength from intertwining their roots with each other, may we as believers support one another in God's vision.

VISION'S REWARD

CHAPTER TWELVE

Be encouraged, running with vision will be rewarded, "For the vision is yet for the appointed (future) time. It hurries toward the goal (of fulfillment); it will not fail" (Habakkuk 2:3 AMP). The race is a marathon, not a sprint. There will be many rewards in life, with the ultimate coveted reward of heaven. "And let us not be weary in well doing: for in due season we shall reap, if we faint not" (Galatians 6:9).

VISION PROMISES REWARD

When the Lord gave me the vision of Cornerstone Church, I saw the glory of God descending from heaven permeating the building. It then reflected in every direction, north, south, east, and west. Instantly, I knew God was saying His glory would radiate from the church to far-reaching areas. It would be a regional church impacting many for the Kingdom of God. We have seen that promise fulfilled in the past 38 years. The Holy Spirit uses people to take His glory to others. Many influencers have carried the anointing of the Holy Spirit to other regions. This influence of the glory and presence of Jesus seems to be intensifying in these last days. The promise the Lord gave you will be fulfilled if you don't quit. You are carriers of the presence of Jesus.

God provides examples of the consequences of quitting in the physical world. An Alaskan expedition was overtaken by a blizzard while searching for their camp. The temperature was plummeting, the snow was deep, and the team was tired. Every step was labored as they forced themselves to press on. One man said to the others, "Let's take a break." Another said, "If we stop, we will freeze to death." They pressed on and eventually agreed to stop. The next morning the blizzard had passed. A search party from the camp was formed to look for the expedition. They were found 100 yards from camp. The team was almost home, but they had quit. Keep pressing on, we are almost home.

We all know the promise in Romans 8:28, "And we know that all things work together for good to them that love God, to them who are called according to His purpose." The problem is we can quote the verse but struggle to live it when times are difficult. In January 2020, the first case of Covid was confirmed in the United States. Most people were petrified with fear of the virus. Some are still in hiding today, five years later.

We as a church overcame the fear and decided to hold on to the promises of God. We chose to believe God was in our midst and would protect us. The Lord gave us a plan of how to minister to God's people. Through daily livestream podcasts, we brought a word of encouragement and hope to many viewers. After stopping in-person services for five weeks we sensed the Lord saying to resume services. Restrictions on people in the worship services were not put in place. We encouraged wisdom, sanitation, and trust in Jesus. Live in faith, not fear. Holding onto God's promises has paid great dividends. In the past three years, we have seen phenomenal growth. Every week, except for one, we have had numerous first-time guests. Hundreds of people have professed faith in Jesus Christ as their Savior. Evangelist Chris Owensby recently told me that Cornerstone has been in revival for the past three years. He said it is a unique revival: steady but consistent. We are humbled by the mighty presence of Jesus. Jesus said, "... lo, I am with you always, even unto the end of the world" (Matthew 28:20). After Jesus ascended into heaven, "They went forth, and preached every where, the Lord working with them, and confirming the Word with signs following. Amen" (Mark 16:20). God is faithful to His Word. We are not working alone; He is working with us demonstrating His awesome power.

There will always be opposition to the rewards of the vision. For years I was concerned about a successor for Cornerstone Church. That concern drove me to pray about the matter for many years. I grew impatient a few times and tried to help the Lord out. Big mistake! It's never pleasant when you create an Ishmael.

However, in my case, the Lord was gracious and chose my successor. In 2007 my son Jamie was gloriously saved. I didn't see that coming and neither did I see him as my successor. Soon Jamie confessed that the Lord was calling him into ministry. In 2007 he began assisting Tim Alexander, our youth pastor.

One year later, Pastor Tim told me it was time for him to hand over the youth group to Jamie and his wife Christy. For the next ten years, Jamie and Christy would serve as youth pastors at Cornerstone. Then Pastor Tim was led to work full-time in missions with Praying Pelican Missions and Jamie began serving as assistant pastor. Fast forward to December of 2023. After Jamie experienced some abnormal symptoms in his body he sought medical attention. He was diagnosed with a mass on his right kidney. Within four days he was scheduled for surgery. On January 24, 2024, the surgeon removed the cancerous kidney. He also removed four lymph nodes; one being enlarged. I think Jamie was on every prayer chain in southeast Ohio. It was a long wait but thank God all tests came back clear, and the Doctor said he was cancer-free. We were praying and believing for that report. The Lord is faithful. The enemy said, "I'll take your successor." He is a liar. When God gives you a promise, the devil is defeated. We are so thankful for everybody that prayed. We couldn't go anywhere for two months without somebody saying they were praying for Jamie. God is good! God gives us staying power no matter what we are going through.

THE REWARD OF KINGDOM WORK

In the early 1990s Pastor Michael Bullock had just pioneered a church in Zanesville, Ohio. He was going through some difficult times and was ready to give up. I saw him after church at a restaurant and invited him to a revival service that night. He promised me he would come. That evening he told his wife Kathy that he was not going to church. Kathy insisted he go because he had promised me. He reluctantly came and stood at the back of the sanctuary wall. The guest preacher was announced and when he approached the pulpit he saw Mike. The preacher began to "read his mail" as well as prophecy to him, "Don't give up, don't quit." Here we are 30 years later, and Mike is still preaching the gospel.

Right after we began to worship in our first sanctuary in 1989, a young man visited on a Sunday night. He came drunk, but God touched him that night. He responded to the altar call. We laid hands on him, and God delivered him. I hadn't seen him for 25 years, but he stopped at the church one day to say thanks. He has never forgotten what the Lord did for him. He is now pastoring a church in Morgan County. He loves Jesus with all of his heart. That is the reward of Kingdom work. It doesn't matter what church a person attends, just so they are saved. We should be willing to help anybody find Jesus and walk out their faith with no strings attached. I have been on the receiving end, too. Dr. Charles Travis has been a dear friend of mine since 1978. When I was in need of help in 1986, he responded gladly to my request for aid. He sent me this email about our encounter:

> "One morning, while pastoring in Ohio, my secretary buzzed me to let me know that I had a call from Pastor Steve Harrop. I quickly took the call because I was aware that he and a co-worker were pioneering a new church at the behest of their pastor and denomination. However, because of no fault of their own, Pastor Steve informed me that their credentials and standing in the denomination had been withdrawn. Here is where the Barnabas anointing comes in, I immediately felt their pain and their anxiety in the precarious situation they

had been put in. We immediately were able to restore their credentials through the authority of our local church, but out of that experience grew a ministry that in just a year would launch Deborah and me into our journey into missions in a broader way than just what we had been doing through the local church. Through that opportunity to serve and assist two brothers in need came the catalyst that launched the forerunner of Logos Global Network... And I want to add that the ministries of those two young pastors have influenced their city and beyond. Now, almost 37 years later Logos Global Network is serving in over 50 nations through its clergy, churches, humanitarian, and community organizations."

Kiddingly, Dr. Travis tells me his ministry is all my fault. The Lord used our need to speak to a man with a heart to help others in need. He is one of the most selfless people I have ever met. It's all about Kingdom vision.

The Cornerstone vision has taken us down a road less traveled. In 2020 the Church of the Brethren asked Pastor Jamie if he would consider pastoring their church. He had preached there several times, and they really liked him. He told them he felt like he should stay at Cornerstone and help his dad. In November of 2020, we mutually agreed to pastor the Church of the Brethren with a team of five ministers on a rotation basis. I had never heard of that being done before, but we thought we'd give it a try. Here we are three and a half years later, and the church has grown. They say they haven't had a bad sermon yet.

In 2023 Ebenezer Church in Roseville, Ohio, contacted our Connect Pastor Eric Waltemire concerning their need for a pastor. Pastor Eric said he was committed to Cornerstone Church but we would be interested in filling their pulpit on a rotation basis. They were reluctant at first, but it has worked well for them, too. The church has grown exponentially. What a joy to serve others in Kingdom work.

Vision can be very rewarding in many ways. We realize that in heaven God will reward the faithful. The greatest reward is to see people come to a personal relationship with Jesus Christ. There is no greater miracle than the miracle of a transformed life. One of the greatest soul- winning endeavors at Cornerstone Church is the Worthy is the Lamb Musical Drama. It presents the story of the creation of the universe, to the creation of Adam and Eve, through the fall of man, to the birth of Christ, His ministry, His crucifixion, and His resurrection. The production is presented three times during the Easter season. Over one hundred twenty people make up the cast and production team. The actors, singers, and tech team are amazing. It is a labor of love that thousands have come to witness. Thousands have been saved over the past thirty-two years.

In 2024 over 4,000 people were in attendance and an estimated 300 people responded to an altar call to receive salvation through Christ's sacrificial death. To God be the glory! Under the direction of our production directors, Pastor Adam Wahl and Brandon Bankes, the Lord has given creative ideas for new scenes and songs that have enhanced the production to a professional level of excellence. This is truly God's reward through His vision to a body of faithful, hardworking, and passionate believers.

LEAVING A LEGACY

Every believer wants to leave a legacy. When we are passionate about Jesus' ministry we can't help but leave a lasting mark in the world. Laikyn's Legacy of Hope has left a lasting impact on our family, our church, and our community (see Chapter 11). In the summer of 2022, we as a church formed teams of two and delivered a bag of hope to over 4000 homes in surrounding townships. In the bag were recovery materials and my book God Has a Man. We are determined to leave a legacy of hope to our world. Laikyn's favorite song was "Different" by Micah Tyler which begins: "I wanna be different, I wanna be changed; Till all of me is gone ..."[35]

I want my life to continue to speak a legacy of hope and faith in Jesus after I'm gone. With the Lord's help and grace, I want to finish my race and be found in Christ. It's not about me and my accomplishments, it's about what He has done through the chiefest of sinners and most unlikely vessel. To God be the glory!

VISION'S HEAVENLY REWARD

Many years ago, a Scottish Evangelist and personal friend,

Howe Davis, left a lasting mark on my life that I will never forget. He was a great preacher, a preacher's preacher. He closed every sermon with the song "It Will Be Worth It All." I want to hear Jesus say, "Well done, thou good and faithful servant: thou hast been faithful over a few things, I will make thee ruler of many things: enter thou into the joy of the Lord" (Matthew 25:21).

Paul said to Timothy: "I have fought a good fight, I have finished my course, I have kept the faith: henceforth, there is laid up for me a crown of righteousness, which the Lord, the righteous judge, shall give me at that day: and not to me only, but unto all them also that love his appearing" (2 Timothy 4:7). Pastor Marvin Johnson, our Visitation Pastor, when talking about a believer that passed away always says, "They have gone on to their reward." The righteous will be rewarded one day. Our greatest reward is being with Jesus forever.

THE REWARD OF LIVES TRANSFORMED

Recently, Charlie and Cindy McCloud invited a gentleman to church at Cornerstone. The Holy Spirit touched him in a remarkable way. He told Charlie he had never felt so clean inside. To hear testimonies of lives changed, families restored, addicts set free, and people being healed of diseases is the greatest reward. Years ago, I saw a documentary about a city in Argentina that had experienced a city-wide transformation. Down every street nine out of ten people were Christians. That is what we are praying for: city transformation.

One of the greatest rewards of a believer is to witness a lost soul come to Jesus. Over the last 38 years, we have seen thousands of souls be born again. Every soul and every conversion is special. One of the most precious, beautiful conversions took place in 1986. A young lady, 16 years old, by the name of Teresa was at the lowest point of her life. She felt empty, isolated, and alone. She battled thoughts of taking her own life but feared the consequences. Teresa had tried many things in the world to find happiness and fulfillment to no avail. A recently saved young man and Teresa's cousin asked to come to her house and share his salvation story. Her mom welcomed them to visit and hear what he had to say about the Lord. Teresa had wanted to know the Lord since she was five years old. However, she felt angry and argumentative with their guests. Two weeks passed and her cousin called to invite her to a newly formed church that was full of life. She accepted the invitation. That morning, she had a sense of elation and expectancy. The service started and Teresa couldn't remain seated. She stood and lifted both hands in the air with great hunger as the presence of God enveloped her. At that moment, all pain, worry, fear, and bitterness left. Her emptiness was filled with the presence of Jesus, His love, and His joys. That day she was born again: a new person in Christ.

Ministers experience a lot of highs and lows. The testimonies of God's transforming power in a lost soul's life keeps me encouraged and motivated to press on. The gospel of Jesus Christ is still the most powerful change agent known to mankind. When I read Teresa's testimony, I knew it would bless and encourage many people. You see, the congregation she referred to was Cornerstone Church in its infancy. We were worshiping in the Philo High School Auditorium. The glory of God was falling. Teresa and her husband, Kenny Campbell, are still serving the Lord in ministry today, 38 years later. My prayer has always been, "Lord, give me souls I can lead to you." At the outset of the vision of Cornerstone, I envisioned pastoring a soul-winning church.

My prayers have been answered. God's people love others so much that they want everybody to know Jesus personally. The prayer that exemplifies the heart of Jesus is Psalm 2:8, "Ask of me, and I shall give thee the heathen for thine inheritance, And the uttermost parts of the earth for thy possession."

The bottom line is vision that does not win souls and disciple believers is out of balance and incomplete. Great will be your reward in heaven as you follow Christ's vision for your life. Our greatest reward is being pleasing to the Father by loving and serving Him with all of our hearts. In the end, we all want to hear Him say, "Welcome home." To God be the glory for His vision!

Our heavenly reward is to see our God who loved us so much that He sent His one and only Son to die for us. He took all of our sins to the cross. That is the greatest love story ever told. To spend eternity with Him and all of our Christian brothers and sisters is my goal in life. Until that day may we lay up our treasures in heaven and be faithful to the Heavenly Vision.

GOD STILL HAS A PLAN!

ACKNOWLEDGMENTS

Very few things in life are done by one individual. Most things require teamwork to make the dream work. God Has A Plan is a combination of many people working together, using their various talents to accomplish this goal.

Thank you doesn't seem to be enough. It's with great appreciation that I extend a heartfelt "Thank You" to all who offered their labors of love. I could never have accomplished this on my own. You have made the dream a reality.

Thank you to my wife of nearly 55 years, Pat Harrop, for her constant support and words of encouragement.

I will forever owe a debt of gratitude to Gail Deitrick, Candy Kelly, and Shelby Wahl for their countless hours of typing.

Special thanks to Gail Deitrick, Mysti Hittle, Dr. Joe & Linda Eichel, Gary Phipps, and Pat Harrop for all their hard work in the editing process.

Also, thanks to Melody Rittberger for her design work on the layout of the book as well as the cover design.

Most of all, I want to thank our Lord and Savior Jesus Christ, for He is the Vision.

SUGGESTED FURTHER READING

Bullock, Michael. (2023). Even Now I Know: A Journey from Greif to Gratitude. Ethos Collective.

Campbell, Kenny. (2022). Bats In The Bell Tower: Unmasking the Doctrines that Have Seduced the Modern-Day Church. Kenneth Campbell.

Ervin, Troy. (2019). Unsinkable Significance. Insight International Inc.

Harrop, Steve. (2021). God Has A Man. Cornerstone Full Gospel.

Pfeifer, Mark W. (2008). Alignment: A Blueprint for the 21st Century Church. SOMA Family of Ministries.

Pfeifer, Mark W. (2007). Breaking the Spirit of Poverty. Morris Publishing.

Pfeifer, Mark W. (2009). Change Agents: How You Can Change Your World. SOMA Family of Ministries.

Thompson, Tom. (2017). A Place of Refuge: A Call from God to Serve Others. Thompson.

NOTES

1. Thompson, Tom. (2017). A Place of Refuge: A Call from God to Serve Others. Thompson.

2. Galloway, D. (D. Galloway, Ed.). (1999). Leading with Vision. (p.9). Beacon Hill Press.

3. Galloway, D. (D. Galloway, Ed.). (1999). Leading with Vision (pp.16-17). Beacon Hill Press.

4. Dew, Doris. "A Dream Come True." 1986.

5. Field of Dreams. Directed by Phil Adlen Robinson, performances by Kevin Costner, James Earl Jones, and Ray Liotta, Universal Pictures, 1989.

6. Biography.com Editors. (2020, April 24) Colonel Harland Sanders Biography. The Biography.com website. https://www.biography.com/busniess-leaders/colonel-harland-sanders

7. Smith, F. (M. Shelley, Ed.). (1997). Renewing your Church through Vision and Planning. (p.196). Bethaney House.

8. Hansen, D. (M. Shelley, Ed.). (1997). Renewing your Church through Vision and Planning. (p.39). Bethaney House.

9. Anderson, L. (M. Shelley, Ed.). (1997). Renewing your Church through Vision and Planning. (p.18). Bethaney House.

NOTES

10. Pfeifer, M. School of Ministry. 203 Equipping the Saints. (p. 17).

11. Hansen D. (M. Shelley, Ed.). (1997). Renewing your Church through Vision and Planning. (p.38). Bethaney House.

12. Johnson, P. (M. Shelley, Ed.). (1997). Renewing your Church through Vision and Planning. (p.261). Bethaney House.

13. Pfeifer, M. School of Ministry. 203 Leadership. (p.15).

14. Valvano, J. (1993, March 4th). [ESPY Awards]. New York City, NY.

15. Foundations for Life. Cornerstone Full Gospel Church (p.4).

16. Pfeifer, M. School of Ministry. 203 Leadership. (p. 17).

17. Galloway, D. (D. Galloway, Ed.). (1999). Leading with Vision (p. 9). Beacon Hill Press.

18. Galloway, D. (D. Galloway, Ed.). (1999). Leading with Vision (p. 11). Beacon Hill Press.

19. Krieger, A. (2021, September 21). EPCOT Was Walt Disney's Radical Vision for a New Kind of City. How Stuff Works.

NOTES

20. Galloway, D (D. Galloway, Ed.), (1999). Leading with Vision (p. 13). Beacon Hill Press.

21. Maxwell, J. (D. Galloway, Ed.), (1999). Leading with Vision (p. 21). Beacon Hill Press.

22. Maxwell, J. (D. Galloway, Ed.), (1999). Leading with Vision (pp. 21-22). Beacon Hill Press.

23. Hunter, J. (M. Shelley, Ed.). (1997). Renewing your Church through Vision and Planning (p.48). Bethany House.

24. Musk, T (M. Shelley, Ed.). (1997). Renewing your Church through Vision and Planning (p.199). Bethany House.

25. Musk, T (M. Shelley, Ed.). (1997). Renewing your Church through Vision and Planning (p. 202). Bethany House.

26. Smith, F. (M. Shelley, Ed.). (1997). Renewing your Church through Vision and Planning (p.192). Bethany House.

27. Kumar, A. (2022, May 16). Study finds 37% of pastors have biblical worldview: Spiritual awakening "needed in our pulpits." The Christian Post. https://www.christianpost.com/news/only-37-of-pastors-have-a-biblical-worldview-barna.html

28. Galloway, D (D. Galloway, Ed.), (1999). Leading with Vision (pp. 120-124). Beacon Hill Press.

NOTES

29. Hunter, J. (M. Shelly, Ed.) (1997). Renewing your Church through Vision and Planning (p. 43). Bethany House.

30. Barnett, T. (1990). Portraits of Vision. Thomas Nelson, Inc.

31. Maxwell, J. (D. Galloway, Ed.), (1999). Leading with Vision (p. 21). Beacon Hill Press.

32. Dunnam, M. (D. Galloway, Ed) (1999). Leading with Vision (p. 149). Beacon Hill Press.

33. Kraby, C (n.d.) Fellowship of the Unashamed: A Martyrs Prayer. Reasonable Theology. https://reasonabletheology.org/fellowship-of-the-unashamed-a-martyrs-prayer/2023

34. "Synergy." Vocabulary.com Dictionary, Vocabulary.com, https://www.vocabulary.com/dictionary/synergy. Accessed 18 Dec. 2024.

35. Lee, K. & Tyler, M. (2016) Different [song]. On Different. Digital EP.

www.ingramcontent.com/pod-product-compliance
Lightning Source LLC
Chambersburg PA
CBHW070737020526
44118CB00035B/1421